L.A.'S ORIGINAL
FARMERS MARKET
COOKBOOK

• MEET ME AT 3rd AND *Fairfax* •

JoAnn Cianciulli

PHOTOGRAPHS BY KARL PETZKE

CHRONICLE BOOKS
SAN FRANCISCO

Library of Congress Cataloging-in-Publication Data available.
ISBN 978-0-8118-5568-6

Manufactured in China.

Designed and typeset by Ph.D, A Design Office

10 9 8 7 6 5 4 3 2 1

Chronicle Books LLC
680 Second Street
San Francisco, California 94107

www.chroniclebooks.com

For my aunt Grace Ragonese,
who taught me the love of books.
Thank you for your lifelong
support and generous spirit.

acknowledgments

Writing cookbooks is quite possibly the most fulfilling job on the planet. I love what I do and am so appreciative for the bounty of blessings that have come my way. Bringing the food of the Farmers Market to life has been an extraordinary experience. This book would not have been possible without the cooperation of all of the restaurant owners and their staff. Thank you for welcoming me into the family and for sharing your recipes and personal stories. You are the true inspiration and the heart and soul of this book.

I am incredibly proud of this project. It is a culmination of patience, time, and hard work, and a number of people gave me vital support along the way. A million thanks to the folks at A. F. Gilmore Company for their confidence and assistance, Hank Hilty, Ernie Mauritson, and Sherif Barsoum, as well as the marketing team of Mark Panatier, Ilysha Buss, Maritza Cerrato, and Michael Hilty for their unwavering encouragement and guidance. I appreciate the expert efforts of David Hamlin and Sydney Weisman for getting the word out and for loving the Market as much as I do. Thanks to Stan Savage for initially believing in the idea and helping make it become reality. Enormous gratitude to archivist Brett Arena for answering all of my annoying fact-checking questions, and to Maryellen Naldjian for always taking such good care of me.

I was extremely fortunate to work with the most creative, energetic, and talented team imaginable. Their contributions are immeasurable and invaluable.

Thank you to top-notch photographer Karl Petzke for saying "yes" in the first place and for being as much fun as he is accomplished. Karl, you are one of the most dynamic people I have ever met and a true master of your craft. Your artistic talent and keen eye perfectly capture the essence of Farmers Market.

Props to Alesha Vanata for taking on recipe testing with me and for always giving her honest opinion. You are a shining light with an impeccable palate and a blast to work with.

To Greek goddess Mara Papatheadoro, whose instinct, wit, and wisdom are nothing short of extraordinary, thank you for taking my words and strengthening them and for helping shape these unique stories. You're an amazing sounding board and this is a better book because of you.

I was privileged to work with the remarkable team at Chronicle Books, which is as smart as they come. Most of all, thank you to my editor Bill LeBlond for believing in me from the start and for ushering me along the way. Additional thanks to project editor Amy Treadwell and designer Anne Donnard for transforming the manuscript into a book. Thank you to Michael Hodgson at Ph.D, A Design Office, for grabbing hold of the challenge and creating a beautiful book.

Great appreciation to my agent extraordinaire Angela Miller for her tenacity and solid advice. You're the best for hanging in there.

Much love to Randall Shaw Andrews for his early contribution to the project and his continuing friendship.

On a personal note, I would like to acknowledge my family and friends for graciously supporting me throughout my career. Thank you for your love without condition, even on those stressful days when I needed a little lift. To my mother and aunt, who are such strong women and role models. And a shout-out to my fabulous group of gals—Shari, Laurie, Kari, Kersti, Rio, Monique, Emily, Deering, and Debbie—I couldn't have done it without you.   — JoAnn Cianciulli

The Los Angeles Farmers Market is filled with one of the most eclectically diverse market communities I have ever witnessed. The opportunity to photograph the Market for this book was a combination of circumstance and luck.

I would like to thank author JoAnn Cianciulli for her prose, dedication, and support throughout the hours and days of photography. Her insight into the individuals and their relationship to the Market brought incredible depth to this project. Many thanks to all the Market vendors who gave their time and portraits to this book. To Alesha Vanata for her many hours of assistance during the long days of food photography. A deep sense of gratitude to our editors at Chronicle Books, Bill LeBlond and Amy Treadwell, for the freedom to create a beautiful book. And finally to Karin and baby Uma who was only two months old when I began this project.   — Karl Petzke

table of contents

foreword

When Farmers Market opened in July 1934, the idea was simple: Farmers from the then-thriving agricultural community in and around Los Angeles were invited to park their trucks on the dirt lot owned by the Gilmores and sell only their best products. They did, and the Market quickly became the place to shop.

Soon after the trucks arrived, crowds ensued, and it became clear that feeding the customers while they shopped was the next step. So, without missing a beat, our merchants did just that. Thus the Market's place in the hearts of locals was forever fixed.

Today, seventy-five years later, Farmers Market continues to offer only the best to its patrons. Whether their products are fruits and vegetables, delicate pastries and delicious pies, bread and cheese, fresh meats, fish and poultry, or the most incredible variety of restaurant fare in all of Los Angeles, the Market's merchants are the best at what they do because they know what their regular customers and visitors from all walks and all distances alike want—high-quality food.

While visiting the Market, you can tour the entire world of good eating. Italy, Japan, Brazil, Mexico, France, China, Korea, Greece, and many other countries—including, of course, the good old USA—are represented. Even with millions of people from around the globe visiting each year, there is something for everyone. In addition to bountiful choices of both prepared dishes and foods ready to cook at home, visitors are treated to the experience of a truly incredible, old-time market at work.

There is a rare spirit of collaboration at Farmers Market; while our grocers and restaurateurs really know their craft, the Market's customers really know what they like, and they do not hesitate to speak up when they think a dish is not quite right or when they have other feedback or ideas.

With this in mind, the entire Farmers Market family hopes that you enjoy reading this wonderful cookbook, with its delicious recipes and behind-the-scenes stories. We hope you take as much pleasure in preparing the dishes as you do in eating them.

Henry L. (Hank) Hilty
President, A. F. Gilmore Company

introduction

These days, all around the country, there are "farmers' markets"—and then there is L.A.'s oldest outdoor market, the Original Farmers Market at Third and Fairfax. From its quaint beginnings in 1934, with local farmers selling produce from the backs of their trucks, to its current spot in the pantheon of Los Angeles's official Historical and Cultural Landmarks, Farmers Market has proven that, indeed, some things really do get better with age. Millions of visitors each year agree.

In its early stages, Farmers Market was a cluster of farm stalls tenanted by small growers who sold directly to the consumer. The main appeal was the extra freshness of vegetables still damp from the morning soil, of fruits ripened on the tree rather than picked hard and green so that they would ship better. The farmers' wives brought in their homemade jams and jellies, and alongside the newly laid eggs and plump fresh chickens were goodies like fresh-baked cookies, homemade breads, and rich chocolate layer cakes, all straight from farm kitchens. It wasn't long before the butcher and grocer sought a place to do business alongside these farmers, who were drawing the patronage of people who knew a good thing when they nibbled it. In time, there appeared import shops and specialty-food stands of nearly every variety. And finally, as a result of an irresistible natural trend, Farmers Market became a cornucopia of restaurants. Today Farmers Market is a combination of family-owned and -operated stalls featuring cuisine, groceries, produce, meats, and seafood from around the world. In a city full of wannabes, where a restaurant is considered a classic if it manages to hang around for more than a decade, the seventy-five-year-old Farmers Market is a miracle of longevity.

Farmers Market is a thriving, ongoing festival of sights and sounds, flavors and smells in the center of our nation's second-largest city. Overlooking one of the busiest corners of Los Angeles, Farmers Market occupies the intersection of Third Street and Fairfax Avenue, supremely anchored in the heart of the city's shopping and dining district.

The original recipes in this cookbook reflect the personality of the Market and represent contributions from every kitchen. Far more than just a collection of weights and measures, this food lover's storybook serves as an enduring companion piece that brings to life the experience that is a trip to Farmers Market. The multigenerational shop owners offer a one-on-one experience that has largely been lost in the service industry today. You can expect to do business with a human being, with a name and a face, who has both stories to tell and your personal satisfaction at heart. In short, the merchants *are* the Market, the faces behind the place. This all-encompassing memoir not only pays homage to their food, but also honors their varied and intense connections to the spirit of this unique place. No matter where you're from, Farmers Market offers a taste of home, as the aromas of several hundred ingredients mingle with the sounds of chatter from several dozen nations. The sense of being welcome and comfortable is evident in the eyes and the smiles of all who visit, be they old or young, veteran or first-timer. This is why the location is so special. It's the reason people gather here. It's why the phrase, "Meet Me at Third and Fairfax" has become an indelible part of the city's lexicon. This is not only a book to cook from, to learn from, to relish; it's one that will re-create the very soul of being at Farmers Market.

The Farmers Market Story

The Original Farmers Market opened on a sunny Saturday at Third Street and Fairfax Avenue in Los Angeles on July 14, 1934. The land on which Farmers Market sits has been in the Gilmore family dating back to the 1870s. When Arthur Fremont Gilmore purchased 256 acres of property, he originally planned to use it for dairy farming, but what was under the soil proved to be much richer. While drilling for water for his herd of dairy cows, A. F. struck oil. By the turn of the century, the dairy was gone, and the Gilmore Oil Company was born. In 1918, the next Gilmore generation assumed control. Earl Bell Gilmore, Arthur's son, went on to turn their independent oil company into the largest in the West, opening many of the first filling stations in the area.

In addition to his acumen for petroleum, E. B. Gilmore was a big sports fan. He built Gilmore Stadium at the corner of Fairfax Avenue and Beverly Boulevard, now home to CBS Television City. The 18,000-seat stadium was host to live sporting events like auto racing, rodeos, football, and boxing. He followed it with constructing Gilmore Field, home of the Hollywood Stars baseball team—owned by Bing Crosby, Barbara Stanwyck, and Cecil B. DeMille. The land, which was christened Gilmore Island, became a gathering place where families could come and enjoy a variety of entertainment.

In 1934, during the Great Depression, an odd pair of dreamers, businessman Roger Dahlhjelm and audacious copywriter Fred Beck, approached E. B. Gilmore with an idea. The two men envisioned a village square where artisans could showcase their handmade goods and local farmers could sell freshly picked produce right out

2

• •

In 1948, presidential candidate Harry S. Truman delivered his famous "stiff upper lip" speech at Gilmore Stadium.

• •

of their trucks. E. B. had a large vacant dirt lot just south of Gilmore Stadium and liked the prospect. Each farmer paid fifty cents rent to park their trucks on the property. According to urban legend, as a PR stunt to lure customers to Farmers Market, Beck painted "Meet Me at Third and Fairfax" on the side of a beat-up truck and feigned car trouble down the street in the intersection of Wilshire Boulevard and Fairfax. The free advertising ploy garnered folks' attention, and the slogan stuck like glue. People came out in droves, and Farmers Market became an instant institution. The atmosphere was like a casual garden party, the open-air commerce enticing, the

products fresh, and the results remarkable. Within the first year, the trucks were replaced by wooden stands with awnings, the food specialty shops multiplied, and there were stores stocked with treasures from around the world. By the 1940s, Farmers Market became a Los Angeles landmark, second only to Hollywood as a favorite place for tourists. Thousands of visitors arrived daily, and the Market grossed more than $6 million annually, earning its reputation as a definitive destination. Little did Dahlhjelm and Beck

A. F. Gilmore   E. B. Gilmore

dream that their impromptu co-op would expand into a bustling commercial center—and the market and dining complex that it is today.

At the turn of the millennium, the one-time dairy farm adapted again. Constructed in the Market's backyard, the Grove opened its doors to L.A. in 2002. Developed by Caruso Affiliated, the shopping and entertainment venue was met with great fanfare and is regarded as the best "mall" of its kind. The complex features stores, restaurants, and a premium movie theater; it has since become one of the most

3

successful shopping destinations in America, drawing an endless stream of consumers every year. It has been said that the Grove attracts more visitors than Disneyland. The outdoor streetscape is inviting, specifically intended for strolling (no car traffic allowed). As with Farmers Market, public spaces are an important component of the Grove—the grandest includes a large, richly landscaped central park with a musical dancing fountain that serves as a major spectacle.

The arrival of the Grove next door has drawn larger numbers of shoppers to the area and represents the Market's new verve. A younger generation of locals and out-of-towners are discovering the wonder and appeal of a leisurely stroll through the Market's labyrinth of stalls and mazelike walkways. Tied to Farmers Market by a gleaming, vintage green trolley and a "Main Street," the Grove has added more attractions to the corner of Third and Fairfax.

For a time though, there were grave fears among the Market's loyal band of diners that the face of progress might also erase the most precious characteristics that have long defined this landmark. Luckily, Farmers Market has always proved to have the inner resources to deal with growing times. The passionate opinions of the Gilmore family, its vendors, and other devout champions prevail, and all parties have

lived to see both a happy ending and a fresh start to the Market's legacy. Not only has the Market thrived, but it has also been reborn, with new tenants reenergizing the established ones. Blending the old with the new, the Market has retained its image as a gathering place and the ultimate town square. Despite the growing pressure to assimilate with modern Los Angeles, things haven't changed much inside the Market. From the original concept to its major renovation and the addition of the Grove, the Market itself remains what it has always been—a delightful and utterly charming place to meet, eat, shop, stroll, and relax, well into the twenty-first century.

Market Mystique

Farmers Market has grown up gracefully with show business as its friend and neighbor. Los Angeles was emerging as the entertainment capital of the world when the Market first opened for business in 1934. Fred Beck states in his 1946 book about the wacky upstart of Farmers Market, *Second Carrot from the End*, that Lou Costello of Abbott and Costello fame was the very first customer, buying a large homemade pickle for a nickel. Hollywood's glitterati have been coming here for years. It's rumored that Walt Disney sat at a Farmers Market table while he sketched the design for Disneyland; and that James Dean ate breakfast here on September 30, 1955, shortly before getting into his Porsche and driving to his untimely death. Gossip columnist Hedda Hopper made it her mission to spot celebrities wandering the aisles and report what they bought. Dubbing the Market "Hollywood's Number One Corner Store," she reported that Greta Garbo shopped here for edelweiss, Charlie Chaplin bought kumquats, and Glenn Ford had a hankering for lemon cream pie. The shine hasn't faded over the years, with Hollywood still calling the Market home. Right next door, a stone's throw away, is CBS Television City. Today, groups of writers, directors, and studio executives gather here for breakfast meetings, and the *Los Angeles Times* lists Farmers Market as a great place to spot celebrities. Perhaps the reason the industry's top players come here is because it is a safe haven where famous faces usually aren't bothered. Much like Mom's house.

The cast of characters who gravitates to this comfortable and friendly oasis contributes to the indulgent act of people-watching, one of the Market's most popular activities. This is a place where people go to retreat and escape the hustle of the surrounding city. In many ways, Farmers Market has become Los Angeles's unofficial break room. A world unto itself, the Market celebrates and welcomes the many quirky and unique elements of the city. It's one of those places you can't describe to New Yorkers. These simple pleasures are what have kept the Market so popular over the years, in spite of its age and the fact that it proudly exemplifies the very antithesis of movie-star chic.

Known for its kitschy barn-style architecture, Farmers Market is made up of a series of white wooden buildings, with green roofs and red shutters. Tenants' stalls are knit together by a network of passageways, creating a maze of narrow, sunny aisles where shoppers can stroll and gaze at the colorful food displays. Each patio breathes its own personality. The array of customers varies dramatically throughout the day, shifting with the changing light, as the sun moves from east to west. From morning regulars to the lunch rush to the cocktail hour and dinner set, the Market's demeanor is in constant flux, all the while retaining its primary identity as a refuge for all who visit.

Basic round tables and folding chairs sit in the center of these open-air aisles, creating a sidewalk café ambiance and offering the opportunity to enjoy the passing parade of humanity. People have long compared the Market, with its intimate scale and specialized shops, to a European market. Others find its atmosphere evokes a sense of an urban county fair, where tourists mingle with studio execs, Russian immigrants from the nearby Fairfax district, and a new wave of trendy Angelenos. The communal meeting ground buzzes with a nostalgic glimpse back to an earlier day, offering an array of sights, sounds, and tastes that have stood the test of time. This enduring gathering spot possesses the perfect amount of neighborhood charm to keep it unpretentious and inviting. Farmers Market has become L.A.'s hip hangout for the casual connoisseur, where both sneakers and pumps can meet for exceptional food.

Farmers Market is special for many reasons. Paramount of these is that it gives people from everywhere—many of whom are immigrants without large financial backing and often with little experience except a desire to contribute to the community—the opportunity to operate a small business. That simple desire is the backbone of our economy and the heart of the American Dream. This book celebrates the foods, people, and history of Farmers Market.

breakfast

As the California sun rises over Third and Fairfax, Farmers Market sprouts to life. The most serene time of day at the Market is when the sounds and smells of morning's glory surround you everywhere. The pace is relaxed, low-key, and unhurried. Although Farmers Market does not officially open until 9:00 A.M., by the time the clock tower chimes 8:00 A.M., vendors are already rolling up the green tarps from their stalls and getting ready for business. The butchers, bakers, and produce purveyors have been here since dawn, long before the sound of the first egg being cracked. Narrow paths front the shops as rays of light stream across the tables and chairs, inviting visitors to come sit, eat, and dawdle. During the week, while commuters are bumper to bumper on Los Angeles freeways, faithful regulars with more flexible schedules begin to trickle into the Market for their morning sustenance. Hollywood is eclectic in so many ways, and Farmers Market reflects that. Families gather for a quality breakfast, folks flying solo enjoy quiet time reading the newspaper, screenwriters tap away on their laptops, and elderly gentlemen congregate on the East Patio to coffee klatch, soaking up the Market's nostalgic atmosphere. Whether you fancy Belgian waffles, delicious baked goods, fluffy omelettes, or crispy fried bacon, Farmers Market is the place to rise, shine, and dine.

BOB'S COFFEE & DOUGHNUTS

STALL
450

Nobody can resist the sweet smell of a doughnut shop in the morning. An L.A. institution and critics' favorite, Bob's Coffee & Doughnuts is an everyday morning pit stop for a long line of Farmers Market visitors. The doughnut shop was first opened in 1948 by a couple remembered as Mr. and Mrs. Arnold, and was, appropriately enough, called Arnold's Coffee Bar & Doughnuts. When the Arnolds put the shop up for sale in 1970, it caught the attention of Bob Tusquellas, who loved the fish business (see Tusquellas, page 191) but wanted to try his hand at something different. Bob put his stamp on the doughnut shop, changed the name, and upgraded the operation, but kept the mom-and-pop traditions alive. Bob's Coffee & Doughnuts prepares twenty-four varieties of deliciously addictive doughnuts the old-fashioned way: by hand. Bob doesn't believe in using new-fangled machinery or conveyor belts; his doughnuts are made with a rolling pin and elbow grease.

You may catch sight of Bob—an early riser known for his friendly manner—serving his sweets and concocting stellar cappuccino in his buttoned-down shirt and crisp white apron. Members of the emeritus generation of the Los Angeles community and other fellow early-rising regulars are often out first thing in the morning, reading the paper and noshing on doughnuts such as honey-glazed and chocolate cream on the East Patio. Bob's makes about one thousand doughnuts on the premises every day, baking in the early morning and again in the afternoon. Customers in the know can set their watches by these shifts, as the alluring smell of fried dough permeates the patio. Bob takes great pride in the popularity of his stand, and credits its success to using the highest quality ingredients to create the perennial perfect combo of coffee and doughnuts. His goal is to bring out the child in everyone and put a smile on their faces with his sweet treats.

11

Caramel-and-Chocolate-Glazed Cake Doughnuts

This recipe is one of Bob's favorites. The tender texture of these cake doughnuts comes from folding in the dry ingredients gently by hand, rather than beating them in with a mixer.

MAKES ABOUT 1 DOZEN DOUGHNUTS; MAKES ABOUT 1½ CUPS EACH GLAZE

Doughnut Batter	½ cup heavy cream, plus more if needed
3½ cups all-purpose flour	Pinch of salt
2 teaspoons baking powder	
1 teaspoon salt	**Chocolate Glaze**
2 large eggs	½ cup (1 stick) unsalted butter
¾ cup granulated sugar	4 ounces bittersweet chocolate, chopped
1 teaspoon pure vanilla extract	2 cups confectioners' sugar, sifted
¾ cup milk	¼ cup boiling water
3 tablespoons unsalted butter, melted and cooled	
	Canola oil for frying
	1 cup finely chopped roasted peanuts (optional)
Caramel Glaze	1 cup rainbow sprinkles (optional)
2 cups granulated sugar	
½ cup water	

To make the doughnut batter: Sift together the flour, baking powder, and salt into a bowl. In a large bowl, whisk together the eggs, granulated sugar, vanilla, milk, and melted butter until well blended. Slowly add the dry ingredients to the egg mixture, stirring just until incorporated into a soft, sticky dough. Cover with plastic wrap and chill for at least 1 hour to make the dough easier to roll and cut. (The dough can be prepared up to 1 day ahead. Keep refrigerated.)

To make the caramel glaze: Combine the granulated sugar and water in a heavy-bottomed pot over medium heat; it should look like wet sand. Swirl the pot over the burner to dissolve the sugar completely. Cook until the sugar melts into a syrup and begins to turn golden, about 5 minutes. Continue to cook until the color deepens to medium amber, about 5 minutes more. Be careful; the sugar is really hot at this point. Remove from the heat and slowly add the cream, a little at a time. It will sputter a bit, so stand back as you pour. When all the bubbling has died down, stir to smooth out the mixture into a medium-thick glaze. Set aside and let cool to room temperature. Mix in additional cream, 1 teaspoon at a time, to thin out the caramel if it gets too thick.

To make the chocolate glaze: Melt the butter with the chocolate in a pot over medium-low heat. Turn off the heat and mix in the confectioners' sugar; it will be very thick and lumpy. Gradually stir in the boiling water to smooth it out. Set aside.

Pour the oil into a countertop deep fryer, cast-iron skillet, or deep heavy-bottomed pot to a depth of about 3 inches and heat to 360°F over medium-high heat.

Turn out the dough onto a lightly floured work surface. Pat and roll out to a thickness of about ½ inch. Using a large doughnut cutter or 4-inch ring cutter (use a smaller ring to cut out the hole), stamp out rounds as close together as possible. Add a couple of doughnuts at a time to the hot oil, keeping an eye on maintaining the oil temperature. Fry until lightly golden, about 2 minutes on each side. As the doughnuts puff up and rise to the surface, flip them over with a slotted spoon, skimmer, or chopsticks. Carefully remove the doughnuts from the oil and transfer to several layers of paper towels or a brown paper bag to drain. Repeat with the remaining doughnuts. Let stand just until cool enough to handle.

Set up an assembly line of the caramel, chocolate glaze, and peanuts and/or sprinkles. First, dip the tops of the doughnuts in the caramel glaze to coat lightly. Dip into the nuts (if using) and then back into the caramel. Finish with a dip into the chocolate glaze. If using sprinkles, dip in the caramel, then in the chocolate, then dip in the sprinkles. Place the doughnuts faceup on a platter or baking pan. Let stand until the glaze is set, about 15 minutes.

13

COFFEE CORNER

STALL
542

A Market gem, this coffee counter has been a mainstay of the East Patio for ages. Established in 1946 by Fred Marconda of Marconda's Meats (see page 155), it was originally an outpost for Manning's Coffee, a popular West Coast coffee chain of that era. Fred's son-in-law Bob Langston took it over in the early '60s and renamed the place Coffee Corner to appeal to a hipper crowd. Bob remained the owner for an astounding thirty-eight years. Current owner Lilian Sears started here as a coffee girl in 1984, when she was only twenty-one years old. In fact, at first Bob didn't want to hire her because he thought she was too young and inexperienced. But Lilian persisted, calling him every day until he acquiesced and gave her a job.

After working for Bob for nine years, Lilian felt she was getting into a rut. She told her boss she was loyal but needed to move on. Bob wouldn't hear of it—she had become like a daughter to him. He struck a bargain with her: If she would stay another five years, he would sell her the place. She stayed and Bob kept his word, offering the shop to her when he was ready to retire in 1998. Lilian didn't have the money to buy the coffee shop and give it a much-needed renovation, so she went to Gilmore Bank, on the Market property, to apply for a loan. The loan officer at the time was a gentleman by the name of Mike Sears. Lilian's loan was approved, and she and Mike started to spend time together during the renovation. Cupid's arrow landed straight in the heart of the Coffee Corner. They were married in 2002.

On an average day, Market visitors purchase more than 1,000 gallons of coffee.

Cappucc
Cappucc
Coffee Corner
Since 1946
rmers Market · 3rd & Fairfax · Los Angele
Espres
Espres

Perfect Cappuccino

Cappuccino is named after the color of the Italian Capuchin monks' robes, which are brown with a white hood. Italians usually drink espresso after dinner, whereas cappuccino is a breakfast beverage, often served with some type of pastry. In the past couple of decades, coffeehouses have proliferated throughout the United States, and cappuccino has gone from "in" to a universally recognized beverage for any time of day. Skim and low-fat milk tend to foam better than whole, but some coffee connoisseurs say you sacrifice flavor along with the fat.

It's best to grind your own beans right before making espresso for the cappuccino. Pregrinding too far in advance affects the taste, texture, and "pull" of espresso. The ideal amount of finely ground espresso to use is 1 ounce per shot. If you don't have a kitchen scale, this is about the same as 1 heaping tablespoon. Owner Lilian Sears stands behind Cuban family-owned Gaviña coffee, but any good-quality bean may be used.

SERVES 1

Whole espresso beans   Cold milk

Using a coffee grinder, finely grind a handful of espresso beans. Put 1 heaping tablespoon of the ground coffee into the basket of the portafilter (the handle with the filtered cup) of a cappuccino machine. (To make a double shot, simply double the grounds.)

Use a tamper or the back of a teaspoon to tamp, or gently pack, the coffee in the basket and get an even surface. The most common mistake of inexperienced baristas is to overtamp, packing the coffee too tightly. This will lead to either bitter or weak shots because the water cannot flow through properly.

Insert the portafilter into the machine, twist to lock, and place a coffee cup underneath. Turn the machine on. A perfect shot of espresso has a very short brewing cycle—only about 20 seconds. It should pour out of the spout in a thick stream, at first very black and then producing a frothy, golden, creamy layer on top, called the *crema*.

To make the foam, it's important to start with cold milk straight out of the refrigerator. Pour the milk into a steaming pitcher (stainless steel works best) until it is about one-third of the way full; the milk will steadily increase in volume while steaming because you are incorporating air into it.

Next, submerge the steam wand into the milk just below the surface. Turn the steam on full power. Adjust the wand so that it is pointing off center in order to get the milk flowing in a rapid, circular motion. Take care to keep the nozzle just below the surface, but avoid letting it come out of the milk, as this will cause splattering and create large, tasteless bubbles. You should hear a hissing noise rather than a rumbling, which indicates that the wand is too deep.

Try to maintain this hissing noise while frothing. You will have to slowly lower the pitcher as the milk volume rises in order to keep the wand tip just under the surface. Steam the milk until a small-bubble "microfoam" is created, giving it a velvety texture like meringue. Look for fairly dense foam with plenty of volume and bubbles that have staying power in a cup. Tap the bottom of the pitcher lightly on the counter to break any large bubbles.

Holding back the foam with a spoon, pour the steamed milk into the cup with the coffee until it is half full. Scoop the remaining foam over the top, heaping it just above the rim of the cup. For a "dry" cappuccino, use less or no milk and only top with foam. For a "wet" cappuccino, add more milk and top with foam.

"When I'm over on this side of town, I grab a double espresso at Coffee Corner. It's a great spot to sit and talk shop with other chefs before we all have to get back to work."
— Joachim Splichal, chef and founder of Patina Restaurant Group

FARM FRESH PRODUCE

STALL
816

The early bird gets the worm—or, in the case of Armando Puente, the happy smiling owner of Farm Fresh Produce, the early bird gets the best pick of produce in town. Three or four nights a week, Armando hits the hay by 8:30 P.M. and hops out of bed at 1:00 A.M. He makes his way along the quiet streets of Los Angeles to the produce district downtown. Typically Armando is first in line to meet up with the farmers and wholesalers, and so secures the prime pick of their seasonal fruits and vegetables. He has a top-quality control policy: Everything he sells is hand-selected by him before it is loaded on the Farm Fresh Produce truck and taken back to Farmers Market. That way, he says, he knows what he's getting and can confidently offer his personal guarantee that the

produce is at the peak of flavor and ready to enjoy.

Armando has earned the trust of not only his patrons but also his peers, as he supplies many of the restaurants at the Market from his fine collection of produce. Armando has been working at the Market since 1989; he became owner of Farm Fresh in 1996. In the mornings, you can see him squeezing fresh orange juice for his customers. The stand features a vintage orange juice machine, circa 1970, that squeezes twenty-five cases of Valencia oranges per day. That translates to about fifty gallons! It doesn't get any juicier than that.

Fresh Fruit Parfait
with Shredded Coconut

In a morning rush? For most of us, breakfast has become somewhat a movable feast, and a refreshing fruit salad is the perfect grab-and-go treat. Farm Fresh Produce makes this rich and beautiful cornucopia of fruit salad every morning and packs it in convenient plastic containers. You can eat it while driving, walking, or relaxing on one of the benches at Farmers Market. The combination of juicy fruit, cool sour cream, creamy condensed milk, and crunchy granola is a great way to start the day.

SERVES 2

½ cup sour cream

½ cup sweetened condensed milk

1 apple, preferably Fuji or Gala, cored and
  cut into chunks

¼ cantaloupe, peeled and cut into chunks

2 bananas, peeled and cut into chunks

4 large strawberries, stemmed and
  halved lengthwise

¼ cup fresh blueberries

¼ cup granola

¼ cup raisins

¼ cup shredded coconut

Combine the sour cream and condensed milk in a small bowl and stir until well blended.

Layer the fruit in 2 parfait glasses or cereal bowls, dividing it equally. Top each with half of the sour cream mixture, then sprinkle each with half of the granola, raisins, and coconut. Serve right away or chill.

¡LOTERÍA! GRILL

STALL
322

Friends and family often tell a particularly excellent cook that he or she should open a restaurant, but even with such support, few have the necessary savvy. However, when loved ones encouraged Jimmy Shaw, eventual founder and executive chef of ¡Lotería! Grill, to go professional with his delectable array of Mexico City street food, he was ready. The Wharton Business School graduate and advertising executive had worked in several restaurants in his day, and also had experience as a private chef. Because of this both felicitous and unusual combination, Jimmy knew how to cook from the heart as well as how to levy his sharp corporate background. ¡Lotería! began as a dream venture, but when the opportunity arose to launch the taqueria

at Farmers Market in 2002, he put the concept into motion and switched career paths. Jimmy explains, "If you're going to do something as crazy as open a restaurant, like I had wanted to for fifteen years, a space at Farmers Market is well worth the risk."

Almost immediately after its launch, ¡Lotería! was recognized as having some of the finest Mexican food available in Southern California, and its charming owner has become another Market success story. Funny thing is, although his name and face say *gringo*, Jimmy Shaw was born and

raised in Mexico City. His goal was to create a place where Mexican expats who live in Los Angeles, like himself, can come to experience nostalgia through food. In the process, with a prime location in the middle of Farmers Market and authentic Mexican fare, his bustling stand became a citywide favorite.

The ¡Lotería! Grill's name was inspired by a beloved Mexican children's card game of chance, similar to bingo but using illustrated pictures instead of numbers. The deck is composed of fifty-four different images; some of the symbols are **EL PESCADO** (the Fish), **EL AMBOR** (the Drum), and **EL MUNDO** (the World). Players shout out "¡Lotería!" ("Lottery!") when they are the winner. The colorful cards have become iconic in Mexican culture and are broadly recognized all over Latin America.

Chilaquiles Verdes

Chilaquiles are a traditional Mexican peasant dish of fried tortillas bathed in green or red salsa (depending on the region) until tender. Slightly tart green tomatillo sauce is preferred in Mexico City, Jimmy Shaw's hometown, and is very simple to make. *Chilaquiles* are most commonly eaten at breakfast time (not uncommonly as a hangover cure). Unlike nachos, *chilaquiles* are a meal to be eaten with a fork. Nothing is wasted in the Mexican home, so this dish was born as a clever way to revive yesterday's tortillas and leftover salsa. At ¡Lotería! Grill you can ask for *chilaquiles* to be topped with a fried egg, *Frijoles Negros* (page 30), or shredded chicken or beef. If frying your own tortilla chips seems too involved (I recommend you try it, though—it's really very easy!), as a shortcut, this dish can be made with store-bought tortilla chips, but choose an unsalted variety.

SERVES 4

Salsa Verde

8 medium tomatillos (about 1½ pounds total weight), husked and rinsed

1 serrano or jalapeño chile, stemmed

½ white onion, halved again

2 garlic cloves

½ bay leaf

Pinch of dried oregano

Pinch of dried thyme

½ teaspoon salt

¼ cup low-sodium chicken broth

1 tablespoon corn oil

Vegetable oil for frying

12 six-inch corn tortillas

2 large eggs, beaten

½ cup shredded Monterey Jack cheese

2 tablespoons crumbled *queso fresco* or mild feta cheese

3 tablespoons finely chopped white onion

1 tablespoon finely chopped fresh cilantro

Crema fresca or sour cream for garnish

To make the salsa verde: Put the tomatillos, chile, onion, and garlic in a medium pot and add water to cover. Bring to a boil over high heat. Reduce the heat to medium-low

continued

and simmer until the vegetables are soft and the tomatillos turn pale green, 15 to 20 minutes. Remove from the heat and let cool slightly.

Carefully transfer the boiled vegetables, along with the cooking water, to a blender. Puree for a few seconds to blend; be sure to hold down the lid with a kitchen towel for safety. Add the ½ bay leaf, oregano, thyme, salt, and broth. Continue to puree until smooth. You should have about 1 quart of *salsa verde*.

Place a wide pot or pan over medium-high heat and coat with the corn oil. When the oil is hazy, pour in the *salsa verde*; it will bubble a bit. Reduce the heat to medium and simmer, stirring occasionally, until the sauce is slightly thickened, 10 to 15 minutes. Cover, reduce the heat to very low, and keep warm while you fry the chips.

Pour the vegetable oil into a heavy-bottomed pot or countertop deep fryer to a depth of about 2 inches and heat to 375°F over medium-high heat. Stack the tortillas and fan them with your thumb to separate. Cut the tortillas into 8 wedges like a pie.

Working in batches, fry the tortilla chips, turning them with a skimmer or slotted spoon so they don't stick together, until golden brown, about 2 to 3 minutes. Remove the chips to a paper towel–lined baking pan or brown paper bag to drain and cool. (Let the oil return to the proper temperature between batches.)

To finish the *chilaquiles*, uncover the *salsa verde* and raise the heat to medium. Just when it starts to bubble, stir in the beaten eggs. Cook and stir for about 5 seconds, until the egg feathers into the sauce, thickening and binding it. Immediately add the chips, tossing gently until they have absorbed enough sauce to become soft. Take care not to break the chips. Sprinkle the Jack cheese on top and let it melt.

Divide the *chilaquiles* among 4 plates. Sprinkle with the *queso fresco*, chopped onion, and cilantro. Garnish with the *crema fresca* and serve immediately.

"There are few things that I crave as much as the *huevos con chorizo* at ¡Lotería! It just hits that note. My wife, young daughter, and I make our way to the Market almost every morning to enjoy a family breakfast."

— Neal Fraser, executive chef/co-owner of Grace and BLD

Huevos Rancheros con Frijoles Negros y Papas con Rajas
(Ranchers-Style Eggs with Black Beans and Potatoes with Pepper Strips)

Huevos rancheros (Spanish for "ranch eggs") are part of many Mexican families' traditions. This recipe was handed down from Jimmy Shaw's mother, Marilyn, who still lives in Mexico City. This is one of the most recognizable dishes on ¡Lotería!'s breakfast menu. The good news is, you can order it all day! On request, they are happy to prepare your eggs scrambled instead of fried. Rich black beans and buttery mashed potatoes round out the meal.

SERVES 4

Ranchero Sauce

3 large tomatoes (about 1½ pounds total weight), quartered

½ white onion, halved again

1 serrano or jalapeño chile, stemmed and halved

1 garlic clove, halved

2 tablespoons corn oil

½ cup low-sodium chicken broth or water

½ teaspoon salt

Vegetable oil for frying

4 large corn tortillas

8 large eggs

¼ cup crumbled *queso fresco* or mild feta cheese

3 tablespoons finely chopped white onion

1 tablespoon finely chopped fresh cilantro

Frijoles Negros (recipe follows) for serving

Papas con Rajas (page 31) for serving

To make the ranchero sauce: Combine the tomatoes, onion, chile, and garlic in a blender (you may need to do this in batches). Blend until completely smooth. You should have about 1 quart of tomato puree.

Place a pot or skillet over high heat and coat with the corn oil. When the oil is hazy, carefully pour in the tomato puree and fry it for a few seconds; it will bubble a bit. Stir in the broth and salt. Reduce the heat to medium-low. Simmer, stirring occasionally, until the sauce deepens in color and thickens, about 30 minutes. Remove from the heat and cover to keep warm while you fry the tortillas and make the

29

continued

eggs. (The ranchero sauce can be prepared a day or up to 2 days ahead; the flavors will only get better. Keep covered and refrigerated and then heat before using.)

Pour the vegetable oil into a large skillet to a depth of about ¼ inch and put over medium heat. When the oil is hazy, add the tortillas, 1 or 2 at a time. Fry until the tortillas are lightly crisped around the edges but still pliable. Using tongs, transfer to a plate lined with paper towels to drain. Repeat until all the tortillas are fried.

Pour off the oil from the skillet and discard. Return the pan to medium heat. Fry the eggs, 2 at a time, just until set.

Dip each tortilla in the warm ranchero sauce to coat and place each on a plate. Put 2 fried eggs on top of each tortilla and spoon over more sauce. The heated sauce will finish cooking the yolks. Garnish with the *queso fresco*, chopped onion, and cilantro. Serve immediately with the Frijoles Negros and Papas con Rajas.

FRIJOLES NEGROS

Frijoles negros (black beans) are a staple of Mexican cuisine. ¡Lotería! features these creamy beans as a side dish, a burrito filling, or on top of *Chilaquiles Verdes* (page 26).

MAKES ABOUT 1 QUART; SERVES 4

2 tablespoons corn oil	1 teaspoon dried *epazote* (see Note)
½ white onion, chopped	1 cup dried black turtle beans, picked
1 tomato, chopped	through and rinsed
2 garlic cloves, chopped	2 cups low-sodium chicken broth
Leaves of 2 fresh thyme sprigs	Salt and freshly ground black pepper

Place a 3-quart pot over medium-high heat and coat with the oil. When the oil is hazy, add the onion, tomato, garlic, thyme leaves, and *epazote*. Cook, stirring, until the vegetables are soft but not browned, about 5 minutes. Add the beans, broth, and enough cold water to cover by 1 inch and bring to a boil. Reduce the heat to medium-low, cover, and simmer until the beans are very tender and beginning to break down, about 2 hours. Watch the heat carefully and stir often to prevent the beans from sticking and burning. Season with the salt and pepper before serving. Serve hot.

Ingredient Note—*Epazote*

Also known as Mexican tea, *epazote* is a native herb with unusually shaped, jagged leaves. Pungent tasting, with a hint of lemon and anise, it can take a little getting used to. It is commonly used in bean dishes because it reduces the amount of gas.

PAPAS CON RAJAS

Rajas means "rags" in Spanish, and in the Mexican kitchen refers to roasted peppers cut into strips. At ¡Lotería! this side dish is popular as a taco filling for vegetarian customers.

MAKES ABOUT 2 CUPS; SERVES 4

2 poblano peppers

1 tablespoon corn oil

2 pounds new potatoes, peeled, halved if large

1 teaspoon salt, plus more for seasoning

½ cup (1 stick) unsalted butter, cut into chunks

Rub the peppers with the oil and roast on a very hot grill, over a gas flame, or under a broiler until the skins are blistered and blackened on all sides. Put the peppers in a bowl, cover with plastic wrap, and let sweat for about 10 minutes to loosen the skins. Peel and rub off the charred skin. Split the peppers, remove the cores and seeds. Cut into ¼-inch strips and set aside.

Put the potatoes in a large pot and cover with cold water. Add the 1 teaspoon of salt and bring to a boil, uncovered. Simmer until there is no resistance when a fork is inserted into the potatoes, about 30 minutes. Drain the potatoes in a colander and return them to the pot. While the potatoes are still hot, mash well with a potato masher. Add the butter and stir vigorously with a wooden spoon. Mix in the poblano strips and season with a generous pinch of salt. Serve hot.

MOISHE'S VILLAGE

STALL
334

With the success of Moishe's (see page 74), owner Movses Aroyan wanted to expand his enterprise. Fortunately, the juice bar next door became available and, in 2003, he converted it into Moishe's Village. At the new sister restaurant, craving the village bread he grew up eating in the Mediterranean, Movses showcases the region's favorite snack food, *boerek*. These savory pastries are easily carried and eaten on the go, and can be filled or topped with just about anything. Though generally thought of as Turkish, *boerek* (also known as *pide*) are commonly found at small cafés throughout Europe.

Movses set out to create a street-corner bakery atmosphere by installing a large, dome-shaped oven as the restaurant's centerpiece.

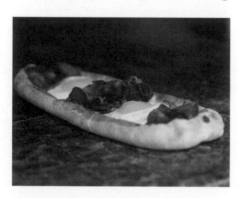

Traditional hearth ovens like this one are lined with ceramic tile and will heat to upward of 700°F. All the *boerek* at Moishe's Village are handmade to order and baked swiftly, right before your eyes. The sight of flames dancing deep inside the oven imparts its own rustic charm for hungry visitors. First-timers may not be familiar with *boerek*, but they usually like what they see. Of course, when people come into Farmers Market, they're willing to try—or often look for—something original.

Boerek

Found in countless cafés in Europe, *boerek* is prepared in almost as many ways; you may find the dough filled and folded over like a calzone or rolled up like a cigar. Regardless of how it's shaped, this rustic bread has an assertive, yeasty flavor with a tender texture. What makes *boerek* more than just bread (albeit very good bread) is what goes on top. At Moishe's Village, spinach and cheese and the ever-popular duo of bacon and eggs are big hits among L.A.'s morning crowd.

Spinach-and-Cheese Boerek

SERVES 4

1 pound fresh spinach, stemmed and finely chopped	¼ teaspoon freshly ground black pepper
2 teaspoons salt	⅛ teaspoon red pepper flakes
½ cup canola oil	1 recipe Boerek Dough (page 37)
1 large onion, finely chopped	1 cup shredded mozzarella cheese
	½ cup crumbled feta cheese

Put the spinach in a large bowl and sprinkle with the salt. Toss with your hands to distribute evenly. Let stand for 20 minutes to allow the salt to draw out the water; the spinach will shrink considerably. Pile the spinach into a piece of cheesecloth or several layers of paper towels and squeeze out the excess liquid. The spinach should be fairly dry so it doesn't make the dough soggy.

Place a large skillet over medium heat and coat with the oil. When the oil is hazy, add the onion. Cook and stir until the onion is very soft and brown, a good 10 to 15 minutes. Season with the black and red peppers (there's no need for additional salt because of the salting and draining step with the spinach). Fold in the spinach, tossing to combine. Remove from the heat. You should have about 2 cups of spinach mixture.

Have ready 4 rolled out pieces of prepared *boerek* dough. Combine the mozzarella and feta cheeses in a small bowl. Sprinkle each piece of dough lightly

35

continued

with 2 tablespoons of the cheese mixture to create a base. Spoon one-fourth of the spinach mixture (about ½ cup) onto each, spreading it out evenly from end to end. Top with the rest of the cheese, about ¼ cup each.

Put a pizza stone or oiled baking pan on the lower oven rack. Remove the other racks to ease access. Preheat the oven and stone or pan to 500°F.

Carefully put 2 of the *boereks* side by side on the hot stone or pan. Bake until the crust is firm and golden, the spinach is hot throughout, and the cheese is melted, 10 to 15 minutes. Cut crosswise into thirds to serve. Repeat with the remaining 2 *boereks*.

Bacon-and-Egg Boerek

SERVES 4

1 recipe Boerek Dough (facing page)
½ cup shredded mozzarella cheese

½ pound bacon slices, cut into thirds,
    cooked until crisp, and drained
8 large eggs

Have ready 4 rolled out pieces of prepared *boerek* dough. Sprinkle the bottoms of each piece of dough lightly with 2 tablespoons of the cheese to create a base. Lay the bacon crosswise in 3 rows on each piece, forming 2 spaces in between for the eggs. Crack 2 eggs onto each boerek, one into each space, taking care not to break the yolks.

Put a pizza stone or oiled baking pan on the lower oven rack. Remove the other racks to ease access. Preheat the oven and stone or pan to 500°F.

Carefully put 2 of the *boereks* side by side on the hot stone or pan. Bake until the crust is firm and golden and the eggs are cooked, 8 to 10 minutes. Cut crosswise into thirds to serve. Repeat with the remaining 2 *boereks*.

BOEREK DOUGH

It's important to note that although this is a yeast dough recipe, the result is much more tender than typical pizza dough with a slight acidic taste from the sour cream. Movses is steadfast that *boerek* is not the same as pizza.

SERVES 4

1 package (¼ ounce) active dry yeast

2 teaspoons sugar

1½ cups warm water

3 cups all-purpose flour, plus more
 for dusting

1 teaspoon salt

2 tablespoons sour cream

1 tablespoon corn oil, plus more
 for greasing

In a small bowl, combine the yeast, sugar, and ½ cup of the warm water; stir gently to dissolve. Let the mixture stand until the yeast comes alive and starts to foam, about 5 to 10 minutes.

Combine the flour and salt in a large bowl or the bowl of standing electric mixer fitted with the dough hook. Add the yeast mixture, sour cream, 1 tablespoon oil, and remaining 1 cup water. Mix until the dough starts to come together and gathers into a ball, a good 5 to 10 minutes. The dough should be sticky and velvety soft.

Turn the dough out onto a lightly floured work surface and knead until it's smooth and elastic, about 10 minutes. Dust as needed with flour to prevent sticking. The dough is properly kneaded when you can pull it and it stretches without breaking. Gather the dough into a ball, place it in a lightly oiled bowl, and turn it over to coat. Cover and let rise until doubled in size, about 1 hour.

When it has risen, knead the dough gently and divide it into 4 equal balls (they should be the size of a large tangerine). Sprinkle the rounds lightly with flour, cover, and let rest for at least 15 minutes so they will be easier to stretch.

On a lightly floured work surface, roll or pat out each dough round into an oblong about 10 inches long and 4 inches wide. (Leave the dough slightly thick, so that the filling will not seep through.) Curl up the edges to create a lip. Top with filling and bake as directed.

PHIL'S DELI & GRILL

STALL
54o

Phil Rice opened his namesake restaurant, originally called Phil's Round-Up, on the east side of the Market in 1973. Phil was from the East Coast and loved a good deli. In 2000, Brazilian transplant Francisco Carvalho took over the credo, and the keys. Francisco was no stranger to the Market. He and his business partner, Cezar Brelaz, owned a successful sightseeing company called L.A. Tours, which brought busloads of hungry visitors to Third and Fairfax daily. Francisco rented an office upstairs at the Market, and as a tenant was on a first-name basis with many of the merchants and their employees. He always had a feeling he would someday run a restaurant in the Market . . . and now he has two (see Pampas Grill, page 171.)

When he was in his early twenties, Francisco was the owner of a local hotspot bar in his native Brazil. While he learned a lot there, his initial experience proved to be more fun than substance. Now that he's more mature, he has found that the restaurant business is his true calling. With his subtle good looks and enchanting accent, Francisco can often be spotted shaking hands and chatting with regulars at the Market. Phil's Deli & Grill offers a no-frills atmosphere, with counter seating that is both casual and inviting. It opens early, around 7:00 A.M., when the Market is just waking up. The menu has basically stayed the same since its beginning. The food comes out fast, just as you ordered it, and the guys behind the grill are happy at work. The place is full of locals, but by the end of your meal you'll feel like one, too!

Pastrami-and-Swiss Omelette

Phil's Deli & Grill brings a little New York style to the City of Angels with tasty cold cuts and Big Apple–size omelettes. The classic trio of hot pastrami, melted Swiss, and grilled rye find their way out of a typical sandwich and into a hearty morning meal that will keep you satisfied and fueled up.

SERVES 2

6 large eggs	¼ pound thinly sliced pastrami, warmed
2 tablespoons milk	and chopped
1 teaspoon kosher salt	½ cup shredded Swiss cheese
½ teaspoon freshly ground black pepper	Toasted rye bread for serving

In a bowl, whisk together the eggs, milk, salt, and pepper.

Place a 9-inch nonstick skillet over medium heat and coat lightly with nonstick cooking spray. Pour half of the egg mixture into the skillet and immediately start tilting and tipping the pan to spread it around. Using a heatproof silicone spatula, gently scrape the cooked eggs to the center of the pan and let the uncooked liquid flow underneath to coat the bottom of the pan. Cook until the eggs begin to set, 1 to 2 minutes.

Arrange half of the pastrami on one half of the omelette and sprinkle half of the cheese on top. Using the spatula, carefully fold the side with no toppings over to make a half moon. Reduce the heat to low. Cook until the omelette is barely browned on the bottom and soft and moist in the center and the cheese is melted, about 1 minute longer. Transfer to a plate. Repeat with the remaining ingredients to make the second omelette. Serve with the rye toast.

THE SALAD BAR

STALL
424

Health nuts and wholesome wannabes can rest easy about getting their daily fill of fresh fruits and vegetables when eating at the Salad Bar. Owner Maria Brown, who bought the business in 1996, has never worked anywhere else in her entire life except at Farmers Market. She arrived in Los Angeles at age thirteen with limited English-speaking skills, but had the will and the commitment to work hard and learn the language. One of fourteen children, she says food is in her blood. Her father was a soda distributor in Mexico, her sister owns a meat market, and it was her brother-in-law who worked at the Market first and got her a job at the place she was most comfortable with: the taqueria Castillo (now home to ¡Lotería! Grill, see page 22). Coincidentally, she ended up just about where she started, as the Mexican eatery is directly across from the Salad Bar.

Today, the splendors of her salads and sandwiches abound and the sensation of her spectacular smoothies beckons. Customers, including TV stars from CBS Studios next door, flock to this popular haunt to place their custom-made orders, mixing and matching combinations of veggies and/or fruits. Carrots are in big demand—over fifty pounds are juiced every day—while on the fruit front, berries top the list. Whether on a plate or in a glass, eating well has never tasted so good. And that is the delicious secret of the Salad Bar and Maria's well-deserved success. It's a long, healthy, and happy way from the barrio of Guadalajara for a little girl with a big, delicious dream.

Mango Delight Smoothie

For the Los Angeles health-conscious culture—from yoga instructors to skate-boarders to beauty queens—the Salad Bar is the place for fast, fresh selections, including a rainbow of custom-blended whole-fruit smoothies. Mangoes' sweet, colorful flesh makes a super-refreshing smoothie that is low in fat and full of flavor. Also a vitamin-C powerhouse, this well-loved tropical fruit is the perfect choice for a simple beverage that packs a nutritional punch, making it the ultimate rejuvenator, whether enjoyed during breakfast or as a mid-afternoon snack. Some customers personalize the drink by adding coconut milk for a colada-style shake.

SERVES 2

1 ripe mango, peeled, pitted, and
   coarsely chopped

1 cup water

½ ripe papaya, peeled, seeded, and
   coarsely chopped

1 ripe banana, peeled and sliced

6 strawberries, stemmed and halved

2 cups ice cubes

In a blender, combine the mango and water. Puree until completely liquefied, about 1 minute. Add the papaya, banana, strawberries, and ice. Blend until smooth and very thick, about 2 minutes.

sandwiches and light bites

chapter 2

When the clock in the tower strikes twelve long gongs, all are aware it is high noon at Farmers Market. The morning calm makes way for the lunchtime bustle, where working pros from nearby CBS Television City and other office buildings come to feed and socialize. An industry lunch spot without pretense, the energy shift is nothing short of a transformation. In a matter of minutes, lines begin to form, tables fill up, and people move a bit faster. They don't have time to waste and need to get back to work.

To accommodate the buzzing midday rush, the restaurants and food stands cook at lightning-fast speed to take care of customers, many who come on a near-daily basis. Whether the craving of the day is a sandwich, salad, or sushi, it's all under one roof. In the late afternoon hours, the flow levels off and patrons break out their sunglasses to linger at the Market. The hearty souls of the city come to do a little shopping, enjoy snacks and conversation with friends, pick up some groceries for dinner, and perhaps bask in the sun. The Price Is Right contestants from neighboring CBS "come on down" to the Market after taping to sample the diverse fare and experience its unique charm. With nametags prominently displayed on their shirts, they are easily spotted. People-watching is actually one of the most fun features of dining here.

CHARLIE'S COFFEE SHOP

It is said that behind every great man is a great woman, yet in the case of Charlie's Coffee Shop, behind every great woman is another great woman! Charlie's has been a fixture on the West Patio since 1976, but a lot of nonregulars probably don't realize that the owner, Charlie Sue Gilbert, is in fact a woman—she's the vibrant redheaded gal deftly commanding the grill. As a little girl, Farmers Market was virtually her playground. Her mother, Fern Foster, worked here her entire life and is a bit of a Market luminary. Back in 1945, Fern started as a counter girl at Dana's, which is now Phil's Deli & Grill (see page 38). In the late '60s, Fern transitioned over to this coffee shop. At the time it was owned by Chris Larson and was, aptly enough, called Chris's Coffee Shop. Fern

adored the place, and when it came time for Chris to retire in 1975, she encouraged her daughter Charlie Sue to buy it—which she did. Charlie Sue renamed it, and together she and Fern made quite a team.

Fern's years of experience paid off as she taught her daughter every rope of the business. But Fern never retired; she worked at Charlie's Coffee Shop until she was eighty-six years old, staying young by eating a charbroiled burger every day. Today, the restaurant bug has passed down another generation, and so the chain of great women continues: On most days, you can spot Katie Gilbert multitasking behind the counter, doing mother Charlie Sue and grandmother Fern proud.

47

Philly Steak Sandwich

You don't have to go all the way to South Philadelphia to get a meaty Philly cheese steak; the tradition has made its way to Southern California. Charlie introduced this manly sandwich to her menu at the insistence of her son-in-law, Mark, who was a truck driver. It's one of the most popular to-go sandwiches.

SERVES 4

1 pound boneless beef sirloin

½ teaspoon salt

½ teaspoon freshly ground black pepper

½ teaspoon sweet paprika

½ teaspoon chili powder

½ teaspoon onion powder

½ teaspoon garlic powder

3 tablespoons vegetable oil

1 medium onion, thinly sliced

1 green bell pepper, cored, seeded, and thinly sliced

1 red bell pepper, cored, seeded, and thinly sliced

¼ pound Swiss or provolone cheese, thinly sliced

4 soft hoagie rolls, split, warm

Put the steak in the freezer for 30 to 45 minutes to firm up a bit; this makes it easier to slice very thinly. Using a sharp knife, shave the beef into ultra-thin slices.

In a bowl, combine the steak slices with the salt, pepper, paprika, and chili, onion, and garlic powders. Toss to coat evenly. Cover and marinate in the refrigerator for at least 15 minutes or up to 2 hours.

Heat a cast-iron skillet or griddle over medium-high heat. When the pan is hot, add the oil, onion, and bell peppers. Cook, stirring, until softened, about 5 minutes. Push the vegetables off to one side of the pan.

Add the meat, chopping it up a bit with tongs, and cook and stir until no longer pink, about 2 minutes. Mix the vegetables back in and toss to combine with the meat. Divide the steak mixture into 4 long mounds in the pan or on the griddle, lay the cheese on top, and cook for 1 minute longer to melt the cheese. Pile the cheesy meat mixture into the warm rolls and serve immediately.

CHINA DEPOT

STALL
744

At the end of the East Patio, the China Depot is one of the longest-standing eateries at the Market, although originally it was called the Chinese Kitchen. It was first opened just after World War II by sisters Gladys Lee and Iris Wong. The two women ran it throughout the mid-twentieth century, then, in 1979, passed the lease on to longtime manager Albert Wong. Meanwhile, Manny Chang and his wife, Angie, were operating the busy employee commissary at the neighboring CBS Studios, which they had done since 1974 and would do through 1990. For years, Manny would walk over to the Market to pick up a few boxes of Bob's Doughnuts for the stagehands. Manny craved the homey Chinese food that Albert prepared, and told him he'd love the opportunity to buy the business if Albert ever decided to sell.

Farmers Market has long been a show-biz haven, and one day in 1991, in a fittingly movie-style twist of fate, a producer "discovered" Albert Wong working the counter. As the story goes, Albert had the perfect look for a Chinese character in the action movie the producer was shooting. The time was right for Albert, and so Manny and Angie became proud owners and changed the name to China Depot. Incidentally, Albert Wong has had a fruitful acting career, appearing in more than a dozen action films including *Rush Hour* and *Armageddon*. China Depot is still family-owned and -operated, as is Manny and Angie's other place, Bryan's Pit Barbecue (see page 111) just a couple of stalls down, where their son, David, is the main man at the counter.

Grilled Vegetable Egg Foo Young

All it takes is a few eggs, crisp vegetables, and a little seasoning to make this popular Chinese-American snack food. Egg Foo Young is one of those dishes that was largely popularized in a bygone time, but is still comforting. In fact, China Depot took it off their menu once but so many people requested it, they complied and put it back on. If you peek into the back kitchen, you can see Angie Chang's mama making the pancakes from scratch twice a day. Serve with the thick, rich brown gravy in this recipe; or you can substitute a good-quality teriyaki sauce. But don't skip the drying time for the veggies; for the patties to hold together, it is important that the vegetables are completely dry.

SERVES 4

....

2 cups finely shredded cabbage	Salt and ground white pepper
1 cup bean sprouts	Canola oil for brushing
1 green onion, white and green parts, finely chopped	
	Gravy
1 medium carrot, shredded	1½ cups low-sodium chicken broth
½ small zucchini, shredded	2 tablespoons soy sauce
¼ cup all-purpose flour	1 tablespoon cornstarch
3 large eggs, beaten	⅛ teaspoon ground white pepper

....

Pat all the chopped and shredded vegetables with paper towels to remove any excess moisture. Spread the vegetables out on a baking pan to air-dry for about 1 hour. If you don't have the time, bake the vegetables for 10 minutes in a 300°F oven. They must be completely dry.

Put the vegetables in a large bowl, sprinkle with the flour, and toss with your hands to combine and coat evenly. Season the beaten eggs with a pinch each of salt and pepper. Fold the eggs into the vegetables to bind them. The mixture should look thick and feel sticky, almost like dough and definitely have more vegetables than eggs.

Place a griddle or large nonstick skillet over medium heat and brush with the oil. Set a 4-inch ring mold in the pan and pack it tightly with the vegetable mixture. Remove the ring and make a second patty. (If you don't have a mold, press the mixture into free-form patties about the size of hamburgers.) Remove the ring again and season the tops of the patties with salt and pepper. Cook until the patties are set and the undersides are crisp, 5 to 8 minutes. Flip with a spatula, season again, and cook the second side until browned, about 3 minutes longer. Repeat to make 2 more patties, adding more oil as needed. Set aside and keep warm. (The egg foo young can be made up to 2 hours ahead and held in a warm oven.)

To make the gravy: Combine the broth, soy sauce, cornstarch, and pepper in a pot over medium heat. Bring to a boil and cook, stirring often, until the gravy thickens, about 3 minutes.

Place an egg foo young patty on each of 4 plates. Spoon the gravy over and serve immediately.

DEANO'S GOURMET PIZZA

The passion and hard work that Dean Schwartz, owner of Deano's Gourmet Pizza, has put into his restaurant is obvious after one visit. For over thirty years, Tony's Pizza and Spaghetti lived in this space; it was a great old-school Italian pizzeria. (Owner/paisan Tony Russo learned the ropes from his Uncle Patsy D'Amore, owner of the Market's other NYC-style pizza place [see page 90], on the opposite patio.) Dean bought Tony's in 2005 and embarked on a massive overhaul. It took him over a year to renovate the aging unit. Fortunately, Dean not only knows his pizza but is also a licensed contractor. The transformation was extensive: he revamped the architecture, replaced all of the fixtures and equipment, and engineered the physical construction. The result is a modern pizza parlor with an art deco feel.

Dean brings a similar artistic focus to the construction of his pizza pies, using the crust as a canvas to create innovative pizza masterpieces ranging from the traditional to the avant-garde. The menu also features delectable pastas and a variety of grilled fare geared to lighter tastes. More and more, customers appreciate dishes that offer flavorful combinations while also satisfying their desire to know that their food is good for them. Contrary to yesterday's rules for the diet-conscious, pizza can be quite a healthful way to eat—and that's something Dean loves having fun with.

Mediterranean Pizza

Simply saying the word "Mediterranean" conjures a wealth of tasty possibilities for pizza. The palette of ingredients is as colorful and rich in variety as the countries that make up the region itself. Dean created a wonderfully thin, fennel-scented crust that's crisp at the edges and bursts with dynamic flavors. If you haven't tried making your own pizza yet, or find it daunting, let this one be your entry to the simple art. Loaded with vegetables, it remains one of the most popular choices for folks who crave pizza but are watching their waistline.

MAKES 1 LARGE (14-INCH) PIZZA OR 2 INDIVIDUAL (8-INCH) PIZZAS; SERVES 2 TO 4

Herb Crust

½ package (¼ ounce) active dry yeast

1 tablespoon sugar

¾ cup warm water

2 cups all-purpose flour, plus more
    for dusting

1 teaspoon salt

1 teaspoon granulated garlic

1 teaspoon Italian seasoning

16 whole fennel seeds (about
    ⅛ teaspoon)

1 tablespoon olive oil, plus more
    for greasing

Topping

1 tablespoon olive oil

1 tablespoon minced garlic

4 cups loosely packed spinach leaves,
    tough stems removed

Pinch of kosher salt

¾ cup pizza sauce

4 ounces goat cheese

4 water-packed artichoke hearts, drained
    and cut into eighths

2 plum (Roma) tomatoes, seeded and
    diced

6 pitted kalamata olives, sliced

8 fresh basil leaves, torn by hand into
    small pieces

To make the herb crust: In a small bowl, combine the yeast, sugar, and warm water; stir gently to dissolve. Let the mixture stand until the yeast comes alive and starts to foam, about 5 to 10 minutes.

In a bowl, mix together the 2 cups flour, the salt, granulated garlic, Italian seasoning, and fennel seeds. Make a well in the center and pour in the yeast mixture and 1 tablespoon oil. Stir with a rubber spatula, incorporating more and more flour to form a soft, sticky dough. Turn the dough out onto a lightly floured work surface and fold it over itself a few times. Knead until smooth and elastic, about 10 minutes. Dust with flour as needed to prevent sticking. Gather the dough into a ball, place it in a lightly oiled bowl, and turn it over to coat. Cover and let it rise until doubled in size, about 1 hour. (For advance preparation, cover the dough and let rise in the refrigerator for several hours or up to overnight.) The chilled dough will stretch more easily.

Preheat the oven to 500°F. If using a pizza stone, place it on the rack and preheat with the oven.

On a lightly floured work surface, roll or pat the dough out into a large circle, about 16 inches in diameter and ⅛ inch thick, leaving the edges slightly thicker. (If making 2 individual pizzas, divide the dough in half and shape two 8-inch circles in the same way.) Put the pizza(s) on an oiled baking pan, or use a pizza stone.

To make the topping: In a pot, heat the oil over medium heat. Add the minced garlic, spinach, and kosher salt. Stir to combine, and cook until the spinach is wilted and cooked down, about 5 minutes. Transfer the spinach to a cutting board and chop coarsely. Let cool.

Ladle the sauce on the dough, spreading it all the way to the edges. Roll up the edges, crimping to enclose a bit of the sauce in the crust. Break up the goat cheese into pieces and drop them evenly around the pizza(s). Scatter the spinach over the cheese and decoratively arrange the artichokes, tomatoes, and olives on top.

57

If using a pizza stone, dust a pizza paddle with flour and slide it under the assembled pizza(s) and onto the hot stone.

Bake until the crust is golden and crispy, about 15 to 20 minutes. Shower the basil on top, cut into wedges, and serve.

Strawberry and Spinach Salad

Deano's is famous not only for their tasty pizzas but also for their farm-fresh salads. Spinach and strawberries might sound like an odd pairing, but the resulting salad is colorful and deliciously refreshing. Great for hot evenings in the summer!

SERVES 4

4 cups loosely packed baby spinach leaves, tough stems removed

2 ounces goat cheese, crumbled into chunks

¼ cup toasted walnut pieces

2 tablespoons dried cranberries

3 to 4 tablespoons raspberry vinaigrette

Kosher salt and freshly ground black pepper

8 fresh strawberries, stemmed and thinly sliced

In a salad bowl, combine the spinach, cheese, walnuts, and cranberries. Drizzle with the vinaigrette and season with salt and pepper to taste. Toss the salad lightly to coat.

Divide the salad among 4 small bowls or plates. Fan 2 strawberries on top of each and serve.

THE FRENCH CRÊPE COMPANY

STALL
318

How did a guy born and raised in the Philippines end up owning a French crêperie in Southern California? His is a real-life story of that melting-pot phenomenon in the United States, the likes of which we really do come across time and time again as we hear people have arrived and thrived in this country. In his native Philippines, Edgar Acosta spent most of his career working in luxury hotels that served guests from around the world. When the Persian Gulf War broke out, he was relocated to Kuwait to manage the Dhahran International Hotel, hub of the United States military action Operation Desert Storm. During wartime, Edgar regularly prepared meals for renowned army general Norman Schwarzkopf, who had a fondness for crêpes. After the war ended, the general thanked Edgar for his hospitality by issuing him a United States passport, and he subsequently adopted Los Angeles as his new home.

Upon arriving, Edgar got acclimated working as a cashier at the Kmart directly across the street from Farmers Market. Parisian Stephane Strouk (see pages 82 and 164), owner of the newly established French Crêpe Company, was a frequent customer. The two men got to talking about French food, specifically crêpes, and in 1993 Edgar became his third employee. Shortly after Edgar came on board, Stephane dismissed his previous two cooks because Edgar could do both of their jobs in half of the time. Almost immediately, Edgar grew to be his boss's right hand, learning all of the ins and outs of the business. Their working relationship developed into a friendship, and before long, their families were sharing holidays together. When Stephane decided to pass the torch in 2004, there was no better person to take over than his "little brother."

59

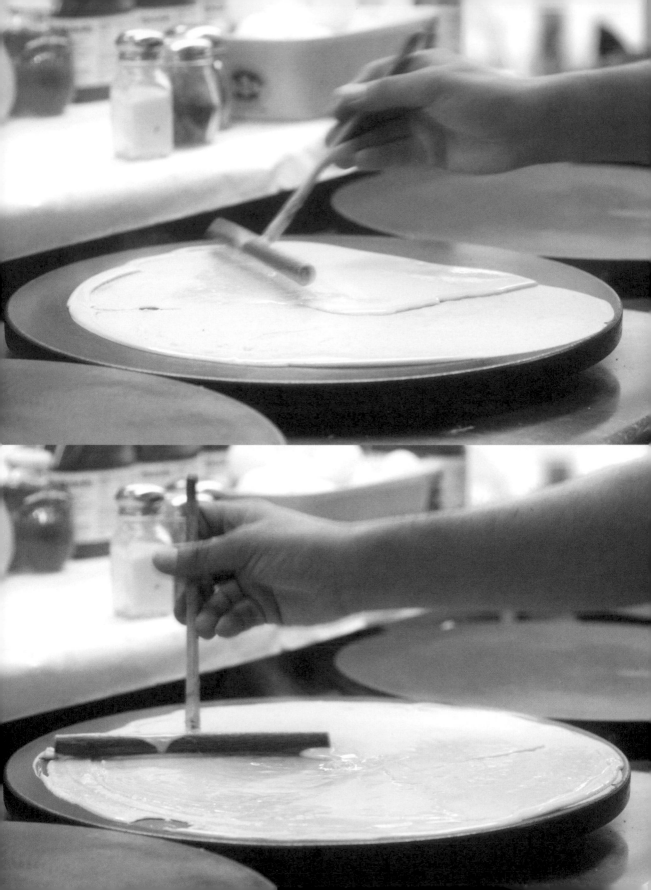

La Normandie Crêpe

As you might imagine, the French Crêpe Company makes magic with crêpe batter. The pancake-like delicacies are amazingly thin and delicate, and the fillings are varied and imaginative. La Normandie Crêpe has been on the menu since Day One. With a saucy chicken-and-mushroom filling, these savory crêpes are one of the most popular for a light lunch and a wonderful change of pace from everyday fare. Serve with a green salad.

Note, it takes a little practice to get the hang of cooking crêpes. Don't be discouraged if the first couple of them end up in the trash.

MAKES 8 (10-INCH) CRÊPES; SERVES 4 TO 8

Crêpe Batter

1 cup milk

¼ cup cold water

2 large eggs

1 cup all-purpose flour

½ teaspoon kosher salt

Unsalted butter, melted,
    for brushing the pan

Sauce

1 cup milk

2 tablespoons unsalted butter

2 tablespoons all-purpose flour

Kosher salt and freshly ground
    white pepper

2 tablespoons Dijon mustard

Filling

2 tablespoons olive oil

1 pound chicken breast tenders, cut into
    ½-inch pieces

Kosher salt and freshly ground
    white pepper

1 carrot, thinly sliced on a diagonal

¼ pound white mushrooms, sliced

¼ pound haricots verts (slender green
    beans), trimmed and cut on the
    diagonal into 1-inch pieces

2 teaspoons chicken bouillon granules or
    chicken soup base

1 cup grated Swiss or Gruyère cheese

61

continued

To make the crêpe batter: Combine the milk, cold water, eggs, flour, and salt in a blender. Blend on medium speed until the batter is smooth and lump free, about 15 seconds. Scrape down the sides of the blender as needed. Let the batter rest in the refrigerator for 1 hour. If the crêpes are made immediately, they have a tendency to be rubbery; when you let the batter stand, they have a better texture and a softer bite.

Place a 10-inch crêpe pan or nonstick skillet over medium heat and brush with a little of the melted butter. Pour ¼ cup of crêpe batter into the pan and swirl it around so it covers the bottom evenly. Cook just until the batter sets and the top appears dry, 30 to 45 seconds. Loosen the sides of the crêpe with a rubber spatula. Turn and cook the other side until pale golden, about 30 seconds longer. The crêpe should be pliable, not crisp, and lightly browned. Slide the crêpe onto a platter. Repeat with the remaining batter to make a total of 8 crêpes, brushing the skillet with more melted butter as needed and stacking the finished crêpes on the platter. Loosely cover the crêpes with a kitchen towel to keep them from drying out. (The crêpes can be made in advance, stacked, wrapped in plastic, and stored in the refrigerator for up to 3 days or in the freezer for up to 1 month.)

To make the sauce: In a small pot, heat the milk to a gentle simmer, stirring so it doesn't scorch the bottom of the pot. Keep the milk on low heat.

Melt the butter over medium-low heat in a 2-quart pot. Just as the foam sub-sides, add the flour, stirring constantly with a wooden spoon or whisk to prevent lumps. Cook the paste for 2 to 3 minutes to remove the starchy taste, but do not let it brown. Gradually add the warm milk, continuing to stir as the sauce thickens. Season to taste with salt and pepper. Reduce the heat and continuing to stir until the sauce is thick enough to coat the back of a spoon, about 2 minutes. Remove from the heat and stir in the mustard. Cover to keep warm.

To make the filling: Place a large skillet over medium-high heat and coat with the oil. Season the chicken pieces all over with salt and pepper and add to the pan. Cook, turning often, until the chicken is lightly browned but not fully cooked, about

5 minutes. Using a slotted spoon, transfer to a plate. To the fat and juices in the pan, add the carrot, mushrooms, and haricots verts; season with salt and pepper to taste. Cook, tossing, until the vegetables are tender and have released their liquid, 3 to 4 minutes. Return the chicken and any accumulated juices to the pan. Add the bouillon. Stir well to combine. Reduce the heat to low and stir in the mustard sauce to bind the filling together. Remove from the heat and let cool slightly.

Place a crêpe pan or nonstick skillet over medium heat and brush with melted butter. Lay a crêpe in the pan and spoon about ¼ cup of the filling along the center. Sprinkle with a handful of the cheese. Using a rubber spatula, fold up all 4 sides of the crêpe so the ends meet in the middle and it looks like a square. Cook for 1 minute to brown slightly. Carefully flip the crêpe over and brush the top with a touch of melted butter. Cook the second side for 30 seconds to heat through. Serve immediately.

Pan Bagnat

Pan bagnat is a popular lunchtime dish in the south of France. Literally "bathed bread," the juices of this tangy tuna salad seep into the bread while it's being pressed. The French Crêpe Company may stand in the middle of the Market, but after sampling this, you'll swear you're in the French Riviera.

SERVES 4

4 ciabatta or demi rolls

2 cans (6 ounces each) solid white tuna, packed in olive oil

1 celery stalk, finely chopped

¼ small red or white onion, chopped

¼ cup sliced, pitted, brine-cured black olives such as kalamata

2 tablespoons drained capers

2 tablespoons chopped fresh chives

1 tablespoon red wine vinegar

½ teaspoon Dijon mustard

Sea salt and freshly ground black pepper

1 small head bibb or butter lettuce, torn by hand into leaves

4 plum (Roma) tomatoes, cut into ⅓-inch-thick slices

1 Persian cucumber, peeled and thinly sliced

2 hard-boiled eggs, sliced

Preheat the oven to 300°F. Arrange the rolls on a baking pan and crisp in the oven for 3 minutes. Remove, and when cool enough to handle, halve lengthwise. Set aside.

In a bowl, combine the tuna and its oil, the celery, onion, olives, capers, and chives. Add the vinegar and mustard; season with salt and pepper to taste. Mix gently but thoroughly to distribute the ingredients.

Layer the bottom halves of the rolls with lettuce leaves. Divide the tuna mixture among the sandwiches, being sure to include a bit of the juice. Top each sandwich with 3 or 4 slices of tomatoes, cucumber, and egg.

Cover with the top halves of the bread and press down firmly. If you have time, put a heavy weight on the top for about 15 minutes to compress the sandwich and allow the juices to sink into the bread. Cut the sandwiches in half before serving.

LIGHT MY FIRE

STALL
230

If you're the type of person who gets fired up about hot sauce, or if you refer to yourself as a "chile head," this hot shop is definitely for you. Owner Young Min is no stranger to peppers, having grown up eating spicy food in her native Korea. When she and her husband, Byoung, opened Light My Fire at the Market in 1998, they stocked a mere two hundred varieties. Today, over a thousand different hot sauces line the walls, literally from floor to ceiling and ranging in price from ninety-nine cents to five hundred dollars. Min jokes that there are countless varietals of wine, why not hot sauce?!

Min manages their inventory very carefully, and seeks out fiery foods from all over the world from Tennessee to Trinidad. In addition to taste, bottle design and the trend in hot sauces for creative, catchy, and outrageous names is a big part of the attraction. There is something for every tongue here, from the banal to the most brutally hot. Everything in the store is rated 1 through 10 on a heat scale, with 1 being mild and 10 hitting off the charts. But in the ring of fire, thrill-seeking hot sauce consumers throw caution to the wind. Min explains that one in five customers comes through the door wanting the hottest thing they sell. In the end, Min gets the most satisfaction from educating customers on her products and answering questions regarding taste, flavor intensity, ingredients, and heat levels. Matching hot sauces to different foods is an art form, and Min is a master at dispensing free cooking advice to her patrons, as well. Min shares the same passion for her love of tea—if she's not at Light My Fire, wander over to her other specialty shop, T Tea Shop (see page 236).

Chicken Wings

If you like wings, Light My Fire boasts a huge assortment of sauces that will take care of every craving you have. From traditional hot-wings sauce to sweet-and-savory blends, these highly addictive potions are extremely versatile and can be added to just about anything. Owner Young Min suggests stirring your favorite wing sauce into dips, dressings, and even burgers or scrambled eggs. Make these on game day and you'll have wing fanatics begging for the recipe.

SERVES 4

20 chicken wings (about 4 pounds total weight)	Wing sauce (your favorite)
	2 celery stalks, sliced into sticks
Kosher salt and freshly ground black pepper	2 carrots, sliced into sticks
	Blue cheese dressing for serving

Preheat the oven to 350°F.

Cut off the chicken wing tips and discard. Split the wings in half at the joint to make wings and drumettes. Pat the chicken dry with paper towels and season generously with salt and pepper. Arrange the wings in a baking pan large enough to hold them in a single layer. Brush the wings with the wing sauce.

Roast the wings for 30 minutes. Turn the wings over and brush the other side with more sauce. Roast until the sauce is baked on and the wings are golden brown, 25 to 30 minutes longer. Preheat the broiler. Slip the wings under the broiler for 1 minute to crisp up the skin.

Serve the chicken wings warm or at room temperature, with additional wing sauce on the side. Accompany with the celery sticks, carrot sticks, and blue cheese dressing.

MAGEE'S HOUSE OF NUTS

For over ninety years, Magee's House of Nuts has been selling the finest assortment of gourmet nuts and nut butters in Los Angeles. Originally opened by Blanche and Ray Magee in downtown's Grand Central Market in 1917, Magee's House of Nuts was quickly recognized for their high quality and superior selection. With their move in 1934, the nut house and Magee's Kitchen (see page 150) became the first shops at the then-new Farmers Market. Phyllis Magee, daughter-in-law of the late founders, married their son Paul in the 1960s. He had been working at Magee's since 1947, when he came out of the service. Phyllis took over the business in 1977. Magee's rich heritage continues today as they maintain an old-world tradition of quality and service.

Phyllis is a stickler for buying only the best and biggest nuts from around the world. The premium-grade cashews are imported from Brazil, the marble-size macadamia nuts hail from Hawaii, and the finest almonds are locally grown right in California. One of the most distinguished claims for Magee's Nuts is that they churn their own fresh nut butters every day. If your timing is right, you can watch beloved employee Doris Perez feed pounds of dry-roasted peanuts into the giant cast-iron grinder. The grinder itself is a relic, built in the early 1900s by Blanche's brother Flavel; it is essentially made out of heavy-duty parts from old farm machinery. The result is a natural peanut butter that tastes rich and pure, with no salt, sugar, or additives. Magee's House of Nuts grinds and sells over 100,000 pounds of fresh peanut butter every year. It's a good thing that they ship across the country.

Spiced Nuts

Fresh, warm, and superior to canned nuts in every way, Magee's wide variety of nuts has been a holiday staple for decades. Whether you're entertaining or serving up homemade gifts, these delicious spiced nuts are essential for a party.

MAKES 4 CUPS

¼ cup (½ stick) unsalted butter

1 teaspoon cayenne pepper

½ teaspoon ground cumin

½ teaspoon ground cinnamon

¼ cup loosely packed light brown sugar

4 cups unsalted mixed nuts such as
  pecans, cashews, pistachios,
  and almonds

1½ teaspoons fine sea salt

Preheat the oven to 275°F. Line a baking pan with aluminum foil for easy cleanup.

In a 3-quart pot, melt the butter over medium-low heat. Add the cayenne, cumin, cinnamon, and brown sugar. Cook for 1 minute to allow the flavors of the sugar and spices infuse the butter. Add the nuts, stirring to coat them completely.

Transfer the nut mixture to the baking pan and spread them out evenly. Bake for about 20 minutes, stirring halfway through, until the nuts are lightly toasted and smell amazing.

Remove from the oven and, while the nuts are hot, sprinkle with the salt. Transfer to a bowl and let cool slightly before serving. The nuts can be stored in an airtight container at room temperature for up to 1 week.

MARKET GRILL

STALL
742

When authentic all-American fare is the desire of the day, patrons head to Market Grill, the unassuming little eatery tucked away in the corner of the East Patio. Juicy grilled hamburgers, plump hot dogs, crunchy fried chicken, and BLT sandwiches with extra-crispy bacon and ripe red tomatoes are all culinary stars, made to order. Golden onion rings, French fries, or their famous fried zucchini on the side balance out the greasy greatness of these delectable classics. For a healthier twist, veggie burgers and grilled chicken have also become menu favorites.

Owner Paula Lau came to Los Angeles from Hong Kong in the late 1980s with her sister, Annie Zou (see Peking Kitchen, page 178). She got her first taste of the Market's flair when she worked part-time for her sister and brother-in-law at their Chinese restaurant. She took to the special ambiance and atmosphere of Farmers Market right away; so when Market Grill owner Scott Bennett decided to sell his stall in 1995, Paula jumped at the chance to work near her family and put into play her impressive skills as a short-order cook. She likes preparing simple straightforward fare, which is why regulars keep coming back for more. Locals from CBS Studios and other offices in the area return day after day for their Americana fix. Those in the know may take advantage of the Market's neighborly spirit—buy a prime steak at one of the Market butchers, Huntington Meats or Marconda's, and Paula will grill it to your liking. So no matter what the request, there is no mistaking the American flavor and hospitality of the Market Grill.

Fried Zucchini

Why just fry potatoes when there is a choice of every vegetable in the garden? These crunchy little coins of zucchini are popular at state fairs and certainly at Market Grill, where the batter is always crisp, very light, and never oily. The irresistible finger food has a little less guilt, because you know you're eating something healthful under there.

SERVES 4

Vegetable oil for frying

½ cup all-purpose flour

2 teaspoons salt

½ teaspoon freshly ground black pepper

2 large eggs

2 medium zucchini, cut on the diagonal
into ¼-inch slices

Ranch dressing for serving

Pour the oil into a large skillet to a depth of 1 inch. Heat over medium heat until it begins to shimmer.

Stir together the flour, salt, and pepper in a shallow plate. In a bowl, lightly beat the eggs. Working in batches, dip the zucchini in the eggs to coat completely and let the excess egg drip back into the bowl. Dredge the zucchini in the seasoned flour, patting to help it adhere on both sides. Place the breaded zucchini slices on a baking pan.

Working in batches, fry the zucchini slices in the hot oil, turning once with a slotted spoon, skimmer, or chopsticks, until golden brown, about 3 minutes per side. Transfer the fried zucchini to paper towels to drain. Serve with the ranch dressing on the side for dipping.

MOISHE'S

Since 1992, Moishe's has been serving authentic Mediterranean and Lebanese specialties to local crowds who can't get enough of them. Founder and owner Movses Aroyan takes a craftsman's approach to cooking: It's not just flavor but also precision and consistency that count. As a former metal engraver and carpenter, he is naturally detail oriented. These values, along with his friendly personality, have played a large part in making him a successful restaurateur.

Always intrigued by the business, Movses believed food was in his soul; and he was spurred on by watching his friends make good money in the culinary world. While living in Montreal, he bought a book on how to run a restaurant and went on a search for the perfect place to call

his own. He found a Canadian-French establishment for sale and liked its character, so he took it over. That must have been some book: the restaurant's profits tripled in six months. Movses had found his calling—and was able to buy his dream car, an Aston Martin.

Sick of the bitter cold Canadian winters, Movses moved to Los Angeles in 1988 and eventually found his way to Farmers Market. This time, with his mother perfecting the fare, he brought to life the delicious and healthful Mediterranean cuisine of his Lebanese roots. To the delight of vegetarians, creamy hum-

mus, golden falafels, smoky baba ghanoush, and tabbouleh salad mixed with fruity olive oil, tomatoes, and lots of parsley all grace Moishe's menu. For his meat-loving clientele, favorites are shish kebabs and the famous rotisserie slow-cooked *shawarma* (thinly sliced shavings of seasoned chicken or lamb) served with hot pita and salad. Customers who stop by soon become regulars, and Movses is always up for a chat.

Falafel Sandwich with Tahini Sauce

Falafel is one of the best-known Middle Eastern "fast foods" in the United States and around the world. Moishe's Lebanese recipe, voted a city favorite, is made with a combination of fava beans and chickpeas (garbanzo beans) that gives the patties a dense, meaty flavor. At Moishe's, they fry them just right: crunchy on the outside and fluffy in the middle, with a nice balance of herbs and spices. Swathed in a pita with lettuce and tomatoes and drizzled with tahini, a tangy sesame sauce, falafel is a tasty lunch alternative to a sandwich or burger. Note, the beans need to soak for at least 12 hours, so do plan ahead.

MAKES 16 FALAFELS; SERVES 4

1 cup dried chickpeas (garbanzo beans), picked through and rinsed

½ cup peeled and split dried fava beans, picked through and rinsed (see Note)

1 small onion, finely chopped

½ small green bell pepper, seeded, deribbed, and finely chopped

¼ cup finely chopped fresh curly parsley

2 teaspoons garlic powder

2 teaspoons ground cumin

1 teaspoon ground coriander

1 teaspoon kosher salt

½ teaspoon freshly ground black pepper

Canola or other vegetable oil for frying

½ teaspoon baking powder

6 pita breads, warmed

Shredded lettuce and sliced tomatoes for serving

Tahini Sauce (page 78) for serving

Pickled turnips for serving

Put the dried chickpeas and fava beans in separate bowls and add cool water to cover by 2 inches. Soak the beans in the refrigerator for at least 12 hours or up to 1 day; they will swell to double their original size. Drain and rinse separately.

Put the soaked chickpeas in a food processor and process until well ground (about the consistency of cornmeal). Scrape the chickpea meal into a large bowl. Process the fava beans in the same way and add them to the bowl with the chickpeas.

Add the onion, bell pepper, parsley, garlic powder, cumin, coriander, salt, and pepper to the bowl. Mix thoroughly by hand until the ingredients are well combined. Refrigerate while heating the oil; this should take about 15 minutes.

Pour the oil into a countertop deep fryer, cast-iron skillet, or deep heavy-bottomed pot to a depth of about 3 inches and heat to 360°F over medium heat.

Add the baking powder to the falafel mixture and toss with your hands to blend. Roll the falafel mixture into 16 balls (about the size of Ping-Pong balls), then press and pat each ball with your fingers to flatten them slightly. Carefully slip a few falafel at a time into the hot oil, using a slotted spoon, skimmer, or chopsticks to make sure they don't stick to the bottom. Fry, turning as needed, until the falafels are crisp and golden on all sides, about 2 minutes per batch. As they are finished, transfer the falafels to a platter lined with paper towels to drain.

To serve, open each pita bread like a book, making sure not to split them completely apart. Scatter a handful of lettuce on one side of the bread, followed by a couple of slices of tomato. Put 4 of the falafels in a row on each top. Drizzle with the Tahini Sauce. Close the sandwiches. Serve immediately, with the pickled turnips.

Ingredient Note—Fava Beans

Fava beans, also known as broad beans, are a staple in Mediterranean and Middle Eastern cuisines. They resemble oversized lima beans with a tough skin that needs to be removed before cooking. Fresh fava beans are seasonal and primarily available in the spring, but dried beans can be found year-round. For ease, look for dried fava beans that are already peeled, sometimes labeled "habas," as peeling the outer shell can be a chore. Dried fava beans can be purchased at natural food stores and international markets.

77

"When I was younger, I used to go with my grandfather to Farmers Market. He liked to visit with all the other older Jewish European men who used to sit and drink coffee and talk politics. Today, I bring my godson there and we always go to Moishe's for the chicken kebab platter, which I think is exceptional."
                    —Josiah Citrin, executive chef/owner of Mélisse

continued

TAHINI SAUCE

Tahini is a paste made from ground sesame seeds, similar to peanut butter. The creamy paste is used in many Middle Eastern dishes such as tahini sauce and hummus (see page 81). It is sold in jars and available at natural food stores, international markets, and most grocery stores.

MAKES ABOUT 1 CUP

½ cup tahini	Juice of 1 lemon
¼ cup plain yogurt	2 garlic cloves, minced
¼ cup water	Pinch of kosher salt

Combine all the ingredients in a blender. Process on high speed to make a smooth and creamy sauce. If it gets too thick as it sits, mix in a little bit more water or lemon juice to thin it before serving.

Vegetarian Platter: Fatoush, Tabbouleh, Spicy Hummus

One of the great pleasures of the Mediterranean table is its innate sense of conviviality, manifested in the tradition of sharing small plates of savory foods. It is a ritual that every country in the region has in common. Known widely as *meze*, these flavorful noshes are typically eaten before the meal or late in the afternoon with drinks at a neighborhood café. The East Patio of Farmers Market is the perfect unrushed, unhurried environment for casual dining with friends. At Moishe's, the vegetarian meze platter is a big favorite.

Fatoush

This vegetable salad uses two unusual ingredients: sumac and purslane. Sumac, usually sold dried and ground, comes from the bright red berries of a wild bush that grows throughout the Mediterranean region. The spice has a delicious, fruity-lemony tang. Purslane is a succulent green plant, whose paddle-shaped leaves are thicker than parsley and have a sweet-sour flavor and chewy texture.

SERVES 4

1 red bell pepper, seeded and chopped

1 green bell pepper, seeded and chopped

2 cucumbers, peeled, halved lengthwise, seeded, and chopped

4 ripe plum (Roma) tomatoes (about 1 pound total weight), chopped

½ white onion, diced

½ bunch fresh curly parsley, finely chopped

¼ pound purslane leaves (optional)

1 tablespoon sumac powder (optional)

Kosher salt and freshly ground black pepper

Juice of 2 lemons

¼ cup olive oil

½ pita round, cut into squares, fried or baked

79

continued

In bowl, combine the bell peppers, cucumbers, tomatoes, onion, parsley, and purs-lane, if using. Toss gently, then season with the sumac and salt and pepper to taste. Moisten with the lemon juice and oil, tossing well. You can set the salad aside at this stage until ready to serve.

Right before serving, add the fried or baked pita squares and mix once more and serve immediately. Keep in mind, fried pita holds up a bit better than baked, which will become soggy more quickly.

Tabbouleh

Movses admits that he treats himself to this classic Lebanese salad every day. The parsley-centric tabbouleh is bright and tangy.

4 ripe plum (Roma) tomatoes (about 1 pound total weight), finely chopped	2 bunches fresh curly parsley, finely chopped
3 green onions, white and green parts, finely chopped	1 tablespoon dried mint
½ white onion, minced	Kosher salt and freshly ground black pepper
½ cucumber, peeled, halved lengthwise, seeded, and chopped	½ cup bulgur wheat (fine-medium grind)
	Juice of 2 lemons
	¼ cup olive oil

In a bowl, combine the tomatoes, green and white onions, cucumber, parsley, and mint. Toss the salad well to incorporate the ingredients; season with salt and pepper to taste. Add the bulgur; moisten with the lemon juice and oil. Fold everything together to evenly distribute the ingredients. The flavor will improve if the tabbouleh sits for a few hours. Serve at room temperature.

Spicy Hummus

Popular in Lebanon and throughout the Middle East, hummus is a creamy puree of chickpeas and tahini (sesame seed paste). It's commonly enjoyed as part of a meze platter with pita bread or vegetable crudités for dipping. Moishe's recipe is a silky, refined version on the lemony, as opposed to garlicky, side.

2 cans (15 ounces each) chickpeas (garbanzo beans), drained and rinsed	½ teaspoon garlic powder
	Pinch of cayenne pepper
1 cup water	1 teaspoon kosher salt
½ cup tahini	¼ cup vegetable oil
¼ cup fresh lemon juice	2 tablespoons toasted pine nuts
1 teaspoon ground cumin	Pita bread, cut into wedges, for dipping

In a food processor, combine the chickpeas, water, tahini, lemon juice, cumin, garlic powder, cayenne, and salt. Puree until very smooth. While the motor is running, pour in the oil and process until fully incorporated, scraping down the sides of the bowl as needed.

Transfer to a serving bowl or platter and garnish with the pine nuts. Serve chilled or at room temperature, with the pita wedges. Store any leftover hummus, covered in the refrigerator for up to 2 days.

MONSIEUR MARCEL GOURMET MARKET

Offering helpful, knowledgeable service, Monsieur Marcel Gourmet Market tempts hungry shoppers with a carefully chosen selection of imported fine foods and private-label groceries. Owner Stephane Strouk was enjoying success with his first business at the Market, The French Crêpe Company (see page 59), when in 1997 he revamped the former grocery store here into a European market. The venture started as a simple cheese shop and, as a *fromage*-loving Frenchman, he was at first his own best customer. As a joke, he named the shop after his father—ironically, Monsieur Marcel hated cheese. The catchy name stuck and fast became associated with the finest cheeses and French delicacies in town.

Stephane expanded the shop's offerings, now featuring a vast selection of fine foods, impressive wines, and top-quality essentials for serious cooks imported from around the world. You will find over twenty-five varieties of extra-virgin olive oils alongside hard-to-find items like white truffles, beluga caviar, and hundred-year-old balsamic vinegars. Stephane and his staff are eager to share their knowledge, and hold wine and cheese classes regularly. Monsieur Marcel Gourmet Market cooks up divine classics for Stephane's nonstuffy French spot next door, Pain, Vin, et Fromage (see page 164). Bistro favorites like custardy quiche, *croque monsieur* sandwiches, and salad *Lyonnaise* are prepared with French flair. Ooh, la, la!

"I know if I need something special, I'll find it at Monsieur Marcel. I love to browse the aisles and sample different cheeses while I'm there. They carry a huge selection of sea salts and ethnic foods like Irish mustard and soda biscuits."
— Ben Ford, chef/proprietor of Ford's Filling Station

Leek and Goat Cheese Quiche

Tangy goat cheese and mellow leeks produce a sophisticated flavor to match the silky texture of this quiche. Monsieur Marcel's quiche changes daily, so check the blackboard at the deli counter for specials. A few steps away, you can find baskets of fresh bread and barrels of ripe olives to complete your French repast. Serve the quiche with a simple green salad.

SERVES 8

1 store-bought refrigerated piecrust, at room temperature

All-purpose flour for dusting

4 large leeks, white and pale green parts only

2 tablespoons extra-virgin olive oil

2 garlic cloves, minced

1 tablespoon fresh thyme leaves, finely chopped

Kosher salt and freshly ground black pepper

3 large eggs

1 cup half-and-half

4 ounces goat cheese, sliced

Preheat the oven to 350°F.

On a lightly floured work surface, roll the pie dough out into a 12-inch circle. Press the dough firmly into the bottom and sides of a 9½-inch pie dish. (Press it into every nook of the pan, especially the edges.) Trim the excess dough around the rim and crimp the edges.

Prick the bottom of the dough with a fork. Lay a piece of aluminum foil on the bottom of the dough and fill it with 2 cups of dried beans. The weight of the beans will keep the pie dough flat so it doesn't bubble while you prebake it. (This is also called "blind baking.") Put the pie dish on a baking pan so it will be easier to move in and out of the oven.

Bake the crust until it begins to brown, about 10 minutes. Lift out the beans in the foil and return the crust to the oven. Bake for 5 minutes longer. Remove the crust from the oven and let cool slightly while you prepare the filling.

Halve the leeks lengthwise and then cut crosswise into ½-inch pieces. Put the sliced leeks in a colander and rinse really well under cool running water, checking for dirt between the layers. Drain well; you should have about 4 cups of sliced leeks.

Place a 10-inch skillet over medium heat and coat with the oil. When the oil is hazy, add the leeks, garlic, and thyme; season with salt and pepper to taste. Cook, stirring occasionally, until the leeks are tender but not browned, about 10 minutes.

In a bowl, whisk together the eggs and half-and-half until frothy; season with salt and pepper. Arrange the leek mixture evenly over the bottom of the crust. Carefully pour in the egg mixture; the filling should come up to about 1 inch from the top of the pie dish. Arrange the slices of goat cheese on top. Bake until the quiche is puffed and set but still jiggles slightly in the center, 25 to 30 minutes.

Remove from the oven and let cool for 10 minutes. Cut into wedges and serve.

Cheese Platter

Monsieur Marcel Gourmet Market is a turophile's heaven, offering more than 250 varieties of cheese from fifteen countries. The best thing about the cheese shop is that they encourage you to taste before you buy! One of the most frequently asked questions is, "What's the best way to put together a cheese course?" The skilled staff's guiding principle is to assemble a selection of contrasting textures and flavors that serve to both please the palate and sharpen hunger. There are no hard and fast rules when it comes to creating an impressive cheese platter. Composing a delectable spread is relatively easy if you follow the cheese experts' advice.

Buying Guide

Select 3 to 5 cheeses that vary in shape, size, and color for a visually attractive platter. Choose an interesting balance of texture (soft, semisoft, hard), flavors (creamy, mild, sharp), and milk types (cow, goat, sheep). So for example, if you choose a semisoft, runny cow's-milk cheese like Camembert, add a supple, strong goat cheese like Humboldt Fog and a hard, gentle sheep's-milk cheese like Manchego. If you're going all out, finish with a pungent blue cheese such as Roquefort. A goat tasting is another great theme—include goat's milk cheeses from several countries, varying in texture and pungency.

Purchase about 1 ounce of cheese per person for appetizers or after dinner; a little more if you're serving less than 5 cheeses.

The Art of Serving

To savor the full spectrum of flavor, always serve cheese at room temperature. Remove from the refrigerator at least 1 hour before serving, keeping it wrapped until you're ready to serve.

Serve cheese on a wood, marble, or granite platter that is large enough to display the cheeses without crowding them. Arrange the cheeses from mildest to

87

continued

strongest, with the cut sides facing out. To avoid mixing flavors, it's ideal to use several cheese knives, maybe one for each type of cheese.

Basic accompaniments can include an assortment of crusty breads and crackers, as well as some palate cleansers (olives, nuts, fresh sliced apples) and flavor enhancers (honey, quince paste, Medjool dates). Think about balancing salty and sweet, spicy and sour, creamy and crunchy. The wine jellies that Monsieur Marcel imports from France add an elegant accent to any cheese platter.

When serving several cheeses at once, one wine will rarely complement all of them. Owner Stephane recommends serving at least 2 varietals—a crisp Sauvignon Blanc and a medium-bodied Pinot Noir will cover many bases.

To store cheese, use wax paper or plastic wrap, but once you unwrap the cheese, discard the wrapping and use fresh for the next storing.

PATSY D'AMORE'S PIZZA

STALL
448

Patsy D'Amore's Pizza is notable for its history—not only is it one of the oldest stands at the Market, it is also widely considered to be L.A.'s first pizza. After having success owning several New York restaurants that featured Neapolitan pizza during the '20s, Pasquale "Patsy" D'Amore and his brother Franklin made the move to the West Coast and opened Casa D'Amore restaurant in Hollywood in 1939. In those days, pizza was not well known, and the trend caught a lot of high-profile attention; Frank Sinatra was a regular customer, and he and Patsy eventually became friends.

Ten years later, the brothers split up and Patsy opened this pizza stand (then called Patsy D'Amores Italian Food) in Farmers Market. Patsy, who had a broad and delightful Italian accent, accelerated the fun and added

drama by tossing his pizza dough up in the air to shape it. He was a showman; when he took the stage on the East Patio, he always drew a crowd.

It seemed everyone in Hollywood loved Patsy's pizza. In its heyday, Patsy's sold over three hundred pies a day! Patsy is gone now, but his daughter Filomena took over the family business in 1998 and still uses the original red-brick oven to create a pizza with a slightly charred, bubbly crust and perfect chew.

"As a kid growing up in L.A., my favorite pizza was Patsy's. I was mesmerized by the enormous gas line that fed the oven; the flame coming out of it looked very dangerous and very professional. I would fold up the bubbling cheese and tomato slice and let the excess oil drip through the waxed paper and onto the paper plate, before taking a giant bite. Heaven!"
— Evan Kleiman, executive chef/owner of Angeli Caffe and host of *Good Food* on KCRW

L.A.'S ORIGINAL FARMERS MARKET COOKBOOK

90

Patsy D'Amore almost got in trouble when pals Frank Sinatra and Joe DiMaggio wanted him to accompany them on a mission to see who Marilyn Monroe was with at a hotel room in town. Patsy didn't want anything to do with it and refused to be an accomplice. But that didn't stop Ol' Blue Eyes and Joltin' Joe. They barged in like gangbusters—but mistakenly broke into the wrong room. A lawsuit ensued, and Patsy was called as a witness to testify against his famous friends. Luckily, folks in Hollywood have a way of forgiving and forgetting, and all charges were later dropped.

Patsy's Special

This eponymous pizza has been on the menu since Patsy D'Amore opened his doors in 1949, when it was a mere twenty cents per slice. Being a great promoter, he wanted to feature a pie loaded with his personal favorite toppings: Italian sausage, pepperoni, mushrooms, and anchovies. This exact dough recipe was originally printed in September 1960 in *Better Homes and Gardens* magazine, hailing Patsy as a "who's who" of Farmers Market. Filomena still uses her father's recipe for Los Angeles's first pizza. The crust produces a very nice floppy New York–style slice that folds perfectly in half. Suffice it to say: if Patsy's pizza was good enough for Sinatra, then it's good enough for you.

If you appreciate the nostalgia but favor the ease of using modern appliances, break out your standing electric mixer (fitted with the dough hook) to make the dough and heat up a pizza stone to bake the pies.

MAKES 2 MEDIUM (12-INCH) PIZZAS; SERVES 8

Dough

1 package (¼ ounce) active dry yeast

1 cup warm water

1 teaspoon sugar

3½ cups all-purpose flour, plus more
    for dusting

1 teaspoon salt

1 tablespoon olive oil, plus more
    for brushing

Topping

1 can (28 ounces) crushed tomatoes

2 teaspoons dried oregano

2 teaspoons dried basil

¼ cup grated Romano cheese

½ pound shredded mozzarella cheese
    (about 3 cups)

¼ pound thinly sliced pepperoni (about
    28 slices)

2 Italian sweet sausages, cooked and
    thinly sliced

½ pound white mushrooms, stemmed
    and thinly sliced

2 teaspoons minced garlic

4 anchovies, minced (optional)

To make the dough: In a large bowl, soften the yeast in the warm water and sprinkle with sugar. Wait a few minutes until the top is foamy. Beat in 1½ cups of the flour to get a dough started, then add the salt and 1 tablespoon oil. Stir in the remaining flour, a little at a time. Knead on a lightly floured surface until smooth and elastic, about 12 minutes. (Dough will be very firm.) Place the dough in a lightly greased bowl, turn to bring greased side up. Cover and let rise in a warm place until more than double, about 1½ hours. It will have a yeasty odor. Let the dough rise until it's as light as a sponge cake.

Punch down, cover, and place in the refrigerator until cold.

Preheat the oven to 500°F. If using a pizza stone (see below), place it on the rack and preheat with the oven.

Cut the dough in 2 parts. On a lightly floured surface, roll each piece of dough out into a 12-inch circle, leaving the edges slightly thicker. Put the crusts on greased cookie sheets or pizza pans, or use a pizza stone, turning the edges of the dough up slightly. Gash the bottom about every 2 inches to prevent bubbles. Brush each crust lightly with oil.

To make the topping: In a bowl, combine the tomatoes, oregano, basil, and Romano. Put a couple of ladlefuls of the tomato mixture in the center of each pizza and swirl around to spread, working outward. Keep a 1-inch border along the edge. Top evenly with the mozzarella, pepperoni, sausages, and mushrooms. Sprinkle with the garlic and anchovies, if using.

If using a pizza stone, dust a pizza paddle with flour and slide it under an assembled pizza and onto the hot stone.

Bake until the cheese has melted and the bottom of the crust is brown and crispy, about 15 to 20 minutes. Repeat to bake the second pizza. Cut into wedges.

SUSHI A GO GO

STALL
434

In a town swimming with sharks, it is no wonder that at feeding time, sushi is big business in L.A. Chef Hiro Funaoku brought his raw talent to Farmers Market in 2001, when he and Janet Nicholson, co-founder and Hiro's American sponsor, opened Sushi A Go Go. On the surface, this low-key hideaway could be any one of the dozens of neighborhood sushi spots in this town. It doesn't have a gimmick or a movie star investor, but its excellence reveals itself in the quality of the food. Designed to satisfy even sushi aficionados, the traditional menu of fresh sushi and sashimi, as well as cooked foods like tempura and udon, is served with stunning presentation and graceful execution.

It's easy to see the ocean in Hiro's blood. Hailing from Osaka, Japan, Hiro grew up in the so-called Water Metropolis. Prized for its supreme fishing, Osaka is bordered by two seas and known for its varied and abundant sushi restaurants. Not surprisingly, when he moved to Southern California, Hiro sunk his toes into the warm sands of Marina del Rey and continued his romance with the sea. An avid mariner, when he's not in the kitchen, he can be found living on his beloved *Aquarius*, a forty-two-feet-long sailboat beauty. Hiro and Janet have won several international yacht races, regattas, and fishing competitions. Once, as they recount the tale, they caught a tuna that was large enough to garner a competition trophy but not pristine enough for Hiro's palate, and he returned it to the sea.

Salmon Tempura Salad with Kiyoko's Dressing

This dish combines the crunch of tempura and the richness of salmon with crisp, cool greens for a light yet remarkably tasteful dish. Hiro's mother, Kiyoko, has been making the simple all-purpose dressing since he was a child.

SERVES 4

Kiyoko's Dressing	Canola or other vegetable oil for frying
1 tablespoon grated garlic	1 cup all-purpose flour, plus about ½ cup
1 tablespoon peeled and grated	for dredging
fresh ginger	¼ cup cornstarch
1 tablespoon sugar	2 teaspoons baking soda
2 teaspoons Japanese hot mustard	1 teaspoon sea salt, plus more for
½ cup rice vinegar	seasoning
½ cup vegetable oil	1½ cups cold seltzer or club soda
Sea salt and freshly ground black pepper	4 skinless salmon fillets (about 6 ounces
	each), cut into strips
	4 cups mixed baby greens

To make the dressing: In a bowl or bottle, combine all the ingredients and whisk or shake until well blended. Store in a sealed container in the refrigerator for up to 2 weeks.

Pour the oil into a countertop deep fryer or deep, heavy-bottomed pot to a depth of about 3 inches and heat to 375°F over medium heat. While the oil is heating, make the tempura batter.

In a large bowl, combine the 1 cup flour, cornstarch, baking soda, and 1 teaspoon salt. Whisk in the seltzer until smooth like a pancake batter and there are no lumps. Pat the salmon fillets with paper towels to remove any excess moisture. Dip the salmon into the batter one piece at a time to lightly but thoroughly coat, letting the excess drip back into the bowl.

Working in batches if necessary to avoid overcrowding the pot, use tongs or chopsticks to carefully lower the salmon into the hot oil. The salmon should sort of fizz when it hits the hot oil and will puff up fairly quickly. Fry the salmon for 2 minutes, then use the tongs or chopsticks to turn the pieces over so they cook evenly, about 1 minute longer. When the coating is light golden brown and crisp, using a slotted spoon, carefully transfer the salmon to a plate lined with paper towels to drain. While the tempura is still hot, lightly season with salt.

Divide the greens among 4 plates. Lay a fillet of salmon tempura on top of the greens and serve immediately with the dressing on the side for dipping.

• •

Occupying a mere 100 square feet, stall #434 is the smallest shop in Farmers Market. It was the original home of The French Crêpe Company (see page 59).

• •

Miso Soup

Drinking miso soup is a Japanese tradition that is still very much alive. With a soothing and mild flavor, it is considered essential for good health and longevity. When drinking miso soup, cup the warm vessel in both hands, allowing the fragrant aroma to steam your face and fill your senses with this superfood. Be "mindful," another Japanese philosophy, as you retrieve the delicate combination of seaweed, tofu, and green onion from the bowl—chopsticks only, please. Serve with the Salmon Tempura Salad on page 96 to complete the meal.

SERVES 4

Dashi (see Notes)

6 cups cold water

3 six-inch pieces dried *kombu* (kelp),
    wiped clean (see Notes)

½ cup shaved dried *bonito* flakes
    (see Notes)

¼ cup dried *wakame* (seaweed)
    (see Notes)

4 ounces firm tofu, cut into ½-inch cubes

2 tablespoons white miso paste
    (fermented soybean paste) (see Notes)

2 green onions, white and green parts,
    thinly sliced on the diagonal

To make the dashi: Combine the water, *kombu*, and *bonito* flakes in a 3-quart pot and place over medium heat. Let the water come to a simmer slowly; this should take about 5 minutes. Turn off the heat immediately just as the stock reaches a boil. Let the stock stand off the heat for 1 to 2 minutes, and then strain out the solids. Use immediately or store, covered, in the refrigerator for up to 3 days.

When you're ready to make the soup, in a pot over medium heat, bring the dashi to a boil. Add the *wakame* and simmer until hydrated and tender, about 5 minutes. Reduce the heat to medium-low and add the tofu. Stir in the miso until dissolved. Remove from the heat. Stir in the green onions. Ladle into small soup bowls and serve immediately.

Ingredient Notes—

Dashi is a basic Japanese soup stock used in many dishes, including miso soup. It is made with dried tuna flakes (*bonito*), kelp (*kombu*), and water. You can find instant dashi in many Asian markets.

Dried *kombu* (kelp) is used extensively in Japanese cuisine and is a key ingredient for dashi. The seaweed is sold dried in sheets in Asian markets and natural food stores.

Dried *bonito* (tuna) is used in Japanese cooking as a garnish and principally in dashi. The tuna is dried, fermented, smoked, and then shaved into delicate flakes. Bonito lends a distinctive strong salty flavor to dishes. Bonito flakes can be purchased in Asian markets and the specialty section of many large supermarkets.

Dried *wakame* is green seaweed that has an ocean-like flavor and slippery texture. Touted for its many healthful properties, *wakame* can be purchased in natural food stores, Asian markets, and the specialty section of some large supermarkets.

Miso paste is the main ingredient in miso soup. Primarily made from fermented soybeans, it is a thick paste that has a salty, almost sweet flavor. White miso is more delicate tasting than the darker colored varieties. Miso can be purchased in Asian markets and in the specialty section of some large supermarkets. Refrigerate after opening.

T&Y (TBILISI & YEREVAN) BAKERY

STALL **222**

The recipe of love, life, and pastry has come full circle for Mike and Rita Davidson, the happily married owners of T&Y Bakery. The couple was fixed up by their families, married only three months after they met . . . and they've been together for over thirty years. Marriage isn't always easy—and neither is baking. But together, this dynamic duo is an example of mixing delicious business with pleasure, flavoring it with a love for each other and the appetite to succeed.

The bakery has always been a family affair. Rita joined her dad at his first bakery in Queens, New York, followed by Mike, who came on board a few years later. In 1991, the warm climate and close-knit ties of the Russian community in Los Angeles brought the family here, where they opened Tbilisi and Yerevan Bakery, which is named after the capitals of Georgia and Armenia (republics of the former Soviet Union), in West Hollywood. After building a strong following, they launched a second location at Farmers Market in 2006. Mike and Rita were delighted when a space became available, because they love the friendly, multiethnic energy of the Market—the mix of old and new traditions, and the blend of locals and international visitors mingling about. In addition to their strong spirit and knowledge of the baking business, the Davidsons just seem to have a lot of fun. On all fronts, the husband-and-wife team has gotten the ingredients and the balance of sweet and savory just right.

Potato Piroshki

Piroshki are probably the best-known Russian hand pies. Like all the incredible baked goods from T&Y Bakery, this recipe comes from Rita's father, Elko Kakiyashvili, and has been in the family for generations. Although T&Y features five different fillings, the traditional potato with dill and caramelized onion continues to be the most celebrated. These piroshki are as authentic as you can get without traveling to Russia. Steaming the potatoes instead of boiling produces the creamiest mashed potato texture.

SERVES 6

Filling	Dough
2 tablespoons vegetable oil	1 package (¼ ounce) active dry yeast
2 onions, chopped	1 teaspoon sugar
4 russet potatoes (about 2 pounds total weight), peeled and quartered	1¼ cups warm water
1 tablespoon finely chopped fresh dill	3 cups all-purpose flour, plus more for dusting
Kosher salt and freshly ground white pepper	2 tablespoons unsalted margarine or butter
	1 large egg
	1½ teaspoons salt
	Vegetable oil for frying

To make the filling: Place a large skillet over medium heat and coat with the oil. When the oil gets hazy, add the onions and cook, stirring often, until soft and lightly colored. Set aside.

Place a steamer basket in a large pot and add water to a depth of 1 to 2 inches. Be sure the water does not touch the bottom of the basket. Cover the pot and bring to a boil over medium-high heat. Put the potatoes in the steamer basket. Cover and

L.A.'S ORIGINAL FARMERS MARKET COOKBOOK

continued

steam until there is no resistance when a fork is inserted into the potatoes, about 20 minutes.

While the potatoes are hot, put them in a bowl and mash well by hand. (Mashing potatoes by hand may be a little more work, but the potatoes will be light and fluffy if you put in the extra effort.) Make sure there are no chunks of potato left. Mix in the dill and cooked onions; season with salt and pepper to taste. Set aside to cool completely. The potato filling may be made up to 1 day ahead and kept in a covered container in the refrigerator.

To make the dough: In a small bowl, combine the yeast, sugar, and ¼ cup of the warm water; stir gently to dissolve. Sprinkle in 1 teaspoon of flour and let the mixture stand until the yeast comes alive and starts to foam, about 5 to 10 minutes.

Put the remaining flour in a large bowl and make a well in the center. Pour in the remaining 1 cup warm water. Add the margarine and break it up with your fingers into the warm water so it melts. Add the egg, salt, and yeast mixture. Mix with your hands, incorporating more and more flour into the center to form a soft, sticky dough. Lightly dust your hands with flour as the dough sticks to your fingers. Take care not to add too much extra flour, however, or the dough will become dense. Turn the dough out onto a lightly floured work surface and fold it over itself, kneading with the heel of your hand, until it's smooth and elastic, about 5 minutes.

Cut the dough into 6 equal pieces and roll into balls; they should be about 4 ounces each (about the size of a cue ball). Sprinkle the rounds lightly with flour. Cover and let rest for at least 30 minutes so they will be easier to stretch.

Pat each dough piece into an oblong about 6 inches long and 2 inches wide. Mound about ¾ cup of the potato filling evenly down the length of each piece, keeping a small border all the way around. Dust your fingers with flour and bring the long edges up to enclose the filling, pinching them together to form a tight seal. Check for any holes or tears, making sure they're completely closed.

Gently pat the piroshki into 8-inch-long pies; they should spread out fairly easily. Turn the piroshki seam-side down and gently pat the tops to spread them out. Lightly dust with flour, cover, and let rise again for about 10 minutes while heating the oil.

Pour the oil into a cast-iron skillet or deep heavy-bottomed pot to a depth of about 3 inches and heat to 375°F over medium heat. Working in batches to avoid crowding the pot, use a wide flat spatula to carefully lower the piroshki into the hot oil. Fry the piroshki on the first side until golden brown, about 2 minutes, then gently turn and fry the other side for 1 minute longer. Transfer to a platter lined with paper towels and let drain. Use more paper towels to blot any excess oil off the tops. Serve warm or at room temperature.

Variation—Oven Method
If you prefer to bake the piroshki instead of frying, arrange them on a lightly oiled baking pan and bake in a 375°F oven until golden brown, about 20 to 30 minutes.

TUSQUELLAS FISH & OYSTER BAR

Masterful attention to detail, impeccable service, and fabulous seafood dishes in a friendly atmosphere is what Tusquellas Fish & Oyster Bar is all about. Established in 1983, Bob opened this fish café as an ideal offshoot of Tusquellas Seafoods (see page 191). The two quite nicely feed off of each other: one place supplies the fish, the other cooks it up to perfection. And after a little seafood, head over to the beloved Bob's Coffee & Doughnuts (see page 11) to take care of that sweet tooth. Bob is privileged to own three stores at the Market, and you never know at any given moment which one you may see him wandering through or plying his many talents.

At this tried-and-true favorite, take note of the specials. The creamy

clam chowder, shrimp salad, and grilled fresh catch (what they have today is what you want today) are all delicious. There are two varieties of fish and chips, and each has fiercely dedicated fans. At lunchtime, locals line up for what they insist is the best tuna salad anywhere in town, period. Part of the fun is taking a peak through the glass window and watching your order being made. Regardless of the choice, satisfaction is delectably guaranteed, and there's nothing fishy about that!

Snow Crab Melt

Bob's take on the classic tuna melt is an afternoon favorite at the Market. The key to this open-faced sandwich is that there is little filler to take away from the sweet, juicy flavor of the crabmeat. Bob points out that it's best to toast the English muffin before assembling the sandwiches. That way, the bread stays crunchy and complements the crab salad—the star of the show. Serve with coleslaw, potato chips, and pickles.

SERVES 2 TO 4

1 pint fresh lump snow crabmeat, picked over for cartilage and shell fragments

2 green onions, white parts only, sliced

1 celery stalk, finely chopped

½ cup light mayonnaise

Dash of hot sauce

Dash of Worcestershire sauce

Sea salt and freshly ground white pepper

2 English muffins, split and toasted

1 cup shredded Cheddar cheese

Preheat the broiler.

In a bowl, combine the crabmeat, green onions, celery, mayonnaise, hot sauce, and Worcestershire; season with salt and pepper to taste. Fold the ingredients together gently but thoroughly, taking care not to mash the crabmeat.

Arrange the English muffins, split-side up, on a baking pan. Top each with one-fourth of the crab mixture and sprinkle with the cheese. Slip the baking pan under the broiler and broil until the cheese has melted, 2 to 3 minutes. Serve immediately.

main meals

Chicken Pot Pie, page 118

In the time of twilight, when the sky glows over Los Angeles and the clock tower illuminates the Market, it signals dinnertime. One of the best things about eating supper at Farmers Market is that it's easy to assemble the meal of your choice. The kids want Italian food. You'd like to have some Chinese. Take a starter from one place, a main dish from another, and go to another stall for a drink. The cross section of cuisine from Brazilian to Greek is almost as impressive as the array of visitors lounging outside at café tables, drinking beer, listening to live music, or belting out songs on karaoke nights. While the idea of driving to a designated spot just to eat, walk around, and be entertained may seem contrived, it's one of the few public spaces in Los Angeles for people to congregate for no other purpose than to enjoy themselves and feel a little more connected. Table service is available at the restaurants, while patios are furnished around the food stalls for casual outside dining. Rain or shine; sunny or cloudy; warm, brisk, temperate, or hot—Farmers Market is open and ready to provide a memorable meal!

BRYAN'S PIT BARBECUE

STALL
740

The Bryan family legacy began with their grandfather, Elias, who began cooking in 1910 in Oak Cliff, Texas. Both Fred "Red" Bryan (who had a gorgeous head of auburn hair) and his brother, William, followed their father into the barbecue business. They cooked in the South Texas–style, old-frontier way: in a pan over wood smoke that slowly permeates the meat with rustic flavor, basting with the natural juices to give the meat a crusty coating. And always in a real brick pit.

The family started their first California location in Studio City, in 1936. When John Gostavitch, Farmers Market's manager, and President Earl Gilmore visited Bryan's Barbecue in 1950 and tasted the great smoke pit flavor, they immediately requested that Bryan's apply for a booth at Farmers Market. It wasn't long before Red Bryan's flavorful smoke was wafting into the nostrils of eager Los Angeles citizens. Red's son, Fred, was always there, as manager and goodwill ambassador, and Fred's children after him. When Red passed away, Fred trained many disciples who aspired to cook the Texas way. Chef Jose Navaro was carver for Bryan's for over twenty years, and Eduardo, one of the first employees, is still working the counter at Bryan's to this day.

The Bryan name remains on the sign at Gate 1, and the barbecue is still delicious, but the restaurant is now run by Manny and Angie Chang, who also own China Depot (see page 51). The wood pit is still the secret ingredient. Fred and his wife, Sheila, now reside in a country club outside of Palm Springs. Life is good there, but they often miss the smell of that old smoky flavored barbecue.

Baby Back Ribs
with Bryan's Barbecue Sauce

It's impossible to replicate the smoky slow-cooked flavor of Bryan's pork baby backs, cooked daily in a giant pit in the back of the restaurant, in a home kitchen. All of their food is served up BIG, with the style and taste of Texas. If you're not from those parts, you're missing out on some good eating. But this home-friendly recipe uses the combination of an oven and a grill to create finger-licking results without a pit or a smoker. The recipe yields about 6 cups of sauce; store leftovers tightly covered in the refrigerator (see Note).

SERVES 4 TO 6

....

Bryan's Barbecue Sauce

1 cup Worcestershire sauce

¼ cup cider vinegar

1 cup firmly packed brown sugar

2 teaspoons fresh lemon juice

1 teaspoon onion powder

½ teaspoon garlic powder

½ teaspoon cayenne pepper

1 teaspoon salt

1 bottle (36 ounces) ketchup

2 racks baby back ribs (about 2 pounds
     each)

Up to 1 cup pan drippings (see Note)

....

To make the barbecue sauce: In a large pot over medium heat, combine the Worcestershire, vinegar, brown sugar, lemon juice, onion powder, garlic powder, cayenne, and salt. Bring to a boil, stirring often to dissolve the sugar. Remove from the heat and set aside to cool a bit. While the sauce is still warm, stir in the ketchup until smooth.

Preheat the oven to 325°F.

Brush the ribs liberally with barbecue sauce, paying special attention to the meaty side. Lay the ribs, meat-side down, in a roasting or baking pan with a rack insert. Pour 2 cups of water in the bottom of the pan; this will make it easier to clean. Cover the pan tightly with aluminum foil.

continued

Bake until the meat begins to pull away from the ends of the bones and the ribs are very tender, about 2½ hours. Discard the foil. Reserve the juices that have collected in the bottom of the pan to use in the barbecue sauce.

Prepare a fire in a charcoal grill or preheat a gas grill to medium-high. Grill the ribs over medium-high heat for 1 minute on each side to char the meat slightly and caramelize the sugar in the barbecue sauce, taking care not to let them burn. (Alternatively, turn the oven up to 500°F and roast the ribs for 5 minutes.) Let the ribs rest for 5 to 10 minutes before cutting them into pieces.

Just before serving, warm 2 cups of the remaining the barbecue sauce and add the reserved meat drippings. Serve the ribs with the warm sauce on the side for dipping.

Ingredient Note—Barbecue Sauce

Fred Bryan believes if you are gonna go take the time to make barbecue sauce, it might as well be a big batch so you always have it handy to fix supper. For the most authentic Texas barbecue flavor, the key is to use meat drippings in the sauce. Fred is so committed to this principle, he keeps a container in the fridge specifically to collect pan drippings from various steaks and roasts. The plain barbecue sauce will keep indefinitely, covered in the refrigerator, but note, once you've added meat drippings, it will only last a day or so.

"I absolutely love the barbecued pork sandwich at Bryan's. The meat is incredibly tender and that smoky sauce is addictive. The service there is great, too. I order the sandwich with coleslaw, a side of baked beans, and a lemonade."

— David Myers, chef/owner of Sona, Comme Ça, and Boule

Glen Ford was a regular customer, as were Mickey Rooney, Cary Grant, Elizabeth Taylor, and many other luminaries in the Hollywood crowd. Joanne Dru and her husband, Woody, who ran a chili cook-off in Texas, were fanatics about Bryan's barbecue sauce, and weekly took pounds of beef and pork home to entertain their Texas friends.

DU-PAR'S

For more than seven decades, Du-par's strong following has enjoyed comfort foods like chicken pot pie and hot turkey with mashed potatoes. Fresh ingredients are a cornerstone of the Du-par's family-style tradition. Every day, they still make fresh squeezed orange juice, grind their own hamburger meat, hand-peel and shred hash browns, and bake fresh homemade pies.

When Du-par's was founded in 1938 by James Dunn ("Du") and Edward Parsons ("Par"), it was a nine-seat stall at the Farmers Market. Eventually Du-par's became a small chain of Southern California restaurants, with other locations in Thousand Oaks and Studio City. In the mid-1970s, longtime executive Herb Oberst assumed ownership of Du-par's; he and his family ran the restaurant for thirty years, until they sold to W.W. "Biff" Naylor in 2004. It's a true testament to Du-par's formula for success that it has only changed hands three times in its history.

Naylor, a food-service veteran for half a century, grew up in the business. His father was restaurant royalty, the man who founded the Hollywood landmark Tiny Naylor's coffee shop eighty years ago. Biff jokes that he came out of his retirement rocking chair to take on the challenge of renovating Du-par's. He saw it as an opportunity to have some fun re-creating the mood of another era. After an extensive two-year overhaul, Du-par's flagship now boasts a twenty-first-century kitchen, '30s- and '40s-style menu, and fully restored 1930s decor, including the original black safe protecting the restaurant's secret pancake recipe.

Biff explains, "Today we're considered cutting edge because we're serving food the old-fashioned way—fresh ingredients, commitment to quality, and taste." For the first time in Farmers Market history, a restaurant is now open 'round the clock at the corner of Third and Fairfax. Biff Naylor has succeeded at making Du-par's a destination for the next generation.

Chicken Pot Pie

The chicken pot pie is a legendary house specialty at Du-par's. It's been on the menu since 1938 (when it cost thirty-five cents) and has not gone out of style. Their old-fashioned recipe, made with whole chicken and freshly cut vegetables, is so good it's not uncommon for them to sell out. Serving individual pot pies makes for a great presentation. You can pick up the crocks or ramekins at any kitchen store if you don't already have them.

SERVES 4

1 small whole chicken (about 2½ pounds)

1 teaspoon kosher salt

3 carrots, diced, trimmings reserved

2 celery stalks, diced, trimmings reserved

1 small onion, diced, trimmings reserved

¼ cup (½ stick) unsalted butter

Freshly ground black pepper

½ cup all-purpose flour

1 large potato, peeled, diced, and cooked (about 2 cups)

¾ cup frozen sweet peas, thawed

2 tablespoons finely chopped fresh flat-leaf parsley

1 frozen puff pastry sheet, thawed (see Note)

1 large egg, lightly beaten with 1 tablespoon water

Put the chicken in a large stockpot and pour in 8 cups of cool water. Add 1 teaspoon of salt along with the reserved trimmings from the carrots, celery, and onion. Bring to a boil over medium-high heat. Simmer, uncovered, until the chicken is just cooked through, about 45 minutes, skimming often as oil rises to the surface. Transfer the chicken to a cutting board to cool. Continue to cook down the chicken stock for another 10 minutes to condense the flavor, until reduced to 4 cups.

Strain the stock through a fine-mesh strainer into a large bowl or measuring cup and discard the solids. When cool enough to handle, shred the chicken meat into bite-size pieces; discard the skin and bones. Transfer the chicken to large bowl.

Preheat the oven to 400°F. Have ready 4 two-cup ovenproof crocks or ramekins.

continued

In a large pot or Dutch oven, melt the butter over medium heat. Add the carrots, celery, and onion; season to taste with salt and pepper. Cook and stir until the vegetables are tender, about 5 minutes. Sprinkle the vegetables with the flour and cook and stir until the flour dissolves, about 2 minutes.

Gradually whisk in the chicken stock, stirring constantly to prevent lumps. Simmer and whisk for 10 minutes until the sauce starts to thicken; it should look like cream of chicken soup.

Mix in the cooked potato, peas, parsley, and shredded chicken. Taste and adjust the seasoning with salt and pepper. Simmer for a minute or so, stirring here and there, until all the ingredients are well combined. Remove from the heat.

Place the puff pastry sheet on a lightly floured surface and unfold it. Using a rolling pin, roll it out slightly. Cut the pastry into 4 equal squares.

Divide the chicken mixture among the crocks or ramekins. Cap each ramekin with a pastry square, pressing the dough around the rim to form a seal. Brush the pastry with the egg wash. Place the pies on a baking pan and transfer to the oven. Bake until the pastry is puffed and golden, about 20 minutes. Let cool slightly before serving.

Ingredients Note—Puff Pastry and Chicken Stock

Frozen puff pastry sheets, readily found in the freezer section of supermarkets, work really well here without compromising the dish. If you are further pressed for time, skip the first step of boiling the chicken. Instead, buy a whole rotisserie chicken from your market deli and a quart of good-quality low-sodium chicken broth. It may not be totally homemade, but the result is very close to the original.

"I LOVE the pancakes at Du-par's . . . in fact, I love most things at Du-par's! The patty melt is great, too, and the waitresses are always really nice and friendly even though they look at me a little funny when I ask for my bacon rare—but they always get it right! I really think their pancakes are the best in town."

— Suzanne Goin, executive chef and co-owner of Lucques and A.O.C.

The pie shop, accessible from inside Farmers Market, sells fresh pies made on the premises with absolutely no preservatives. The dessert kitchen is behind glass so customers can watch bakers prepare the pies as they did years ago.

Welsh Rarebit

Welsh rarebit (sometimes known as Welsh "rabbit" . . . although there are no bunnies in the sauce) is one of those old recipes that you don't see much on menus anymore. Similar to cheese on toast, it is commonly eaten as a savory snack in Britain. At Du-par's, folks enjoy the hunks of toasted bread covered in gooey cheese sauce as a main meal. It is quite filling on its own, but goes very well with a green salad.

SERVES 4

2 tablespoons unsalted butter

1 tablespoon all-purpose flour

1 teaspoon dry mustard

Pinch of cayenne pepper

Pinch of paprika

2 teaspoons Worcestershire sauce

½ bottle (6 ounces) ale

½ pound sharp English Cheddar cheese, shredded

4 thick slices country white bread, toasted

4 slices tomato

4 slices crisp-cooked bacon, crumbled

In a 3-quart pot, melt the butter over medium heat. Sprinkle in the flour and cook, stirring constantly, until the flour dissolves, about 1 minute. Add the mustard, cayenne, paprika, and Worcestershire, stirring to incorporate. Slowly whisk in the ale. When the bubbles subside, gradually add the cheese a few handfuls at a time, stirring constantly, until the cheese melts and the sauce is smooth and creamy.

To serve, place a slice of toast on each of 4 individual plates. Pour the cheese sauce over the toast, dividing it evenly, and garnish each serving with a tomato slice and a sprinkling of bacon. Serve immediately.

FARMERS MARKET POULTRY

Since 1987, Julio Laj's Farmers Market Poultry has earned a reputation for superior quality and taste among leading chefs and discerning customers. The shop carries not only the finest fowl, but also topnotch delicacies such as frog's legs, foie gras, and rabbit.

The store first opened in 1962 as Roger's Poultry. Roger Claus was an expert butcher, and his business grew quickly. He hired Mike Izzarelli, fresh out of the navy and keen to learn the trade, to help. Under Roger's tutelage, Mike found that being a butcher shares a common discipline with the military. Roger trained him to slice, dice, and chop, and passed along a work ethic that Mike embraces to this day: Be fair, be consistent, and be proud of what you do. As a result, Mike treated the store as if

it were his own—and so it was when Roger retired and sold it to him in 1983. Mike became friendly with Julio Laj at the neighborhood restaurant where Julio was the manager and they often shared a drink or two. Intrigued by the butcher business, Julio began working at the poultry counter. It was obvious immediately that Julio had a knack for dealing with the clientele and was dexterous with a butcher knife. So when the time came, knowing it was in hands he could trust, Mike sold Julio the poultry shop.

Julio loves being a Market owner and appreciates the personal pride each proprietor has about their place and their products. Committed to accommodating all desires and requests from organic to free range, he is impressed that his consumers know what they want. And when Julio and Mike get together now, they can still talk shop; while Julio does his slicing and dicing magic at Farmers Market Poultry, Mike works part-time at Marconda's Meats (see page 155).

Seared Duck Breast
with Pomegranate Glaze

Duck, the most succulent of birds, shines in this simple yet sophisticated recipe. With its assertive, rich, meaty flavor, it is an elegant alternative to chicken. Choose a duck breast of any variety available to you—Julio suggests using Magret (from Moulard ducks) or the smaller Muscovy duck breasts. Fine butchers like Farmers Market Poultry carry both. Couscous or wild rice goes nicely with this dish, as does a bottle of good red wine.

SERVES 4

4 boneless, skin-on duck breast halves	1 shallot, minced
Kosher salt and freshly ground black pepper	1 cup pomegranate juice
	2 tablespoons demi-glace (see Note)
1 tablespoon olive oil	Pomegranate seeds for garnish
2 tablespoons unsalted butter	Chopped pistachios for garnish

Score the skin of the duck breasts in a crisscross pattern with a sharp knife; take care not to cut all the way through into the meat. Season generously on both sides with salt and pepper.

Place a large skillet over medium-high heat and coat with the oil. When the oil is hazy, add the duck breasts, skin-side down, and cook until the skin is golden brown and crispy, about 5 minutes. As the fat renders out of the skin, carefully drain it off. Turn the duck breasts over and cook the other side until firm, about 2 minutes longer for medium-rare.

Remove the duck to a cutting board and let rest for 5 minutes while preparing the pan sauce. Pour off the fat from the skillet. Add 1 tablespoon of the butter and melt over medium heat. Add the shallot and stir until translucent, about 2 minutes. Add the pomegranate juice. Cook and stir until the liquid is reduced to a glaze, scraping up any browned bits, about 3 minutes. Add the demi-glace and stir until combined.

Remove from the heat and swirl in the remaining 1 tablespoon butter. Season to taste with salt and pepper.

Carve each duck breast on the diagonal into slices ½ inch thick. Arrange on individual plates and spoon the pomegranate glaze over and around. Sprinkle with the pomegranate seeds and pistachios. Serve immediately.

Ingredient Note—Demi-Glace

Demi-glace is a very rich brown sauce with concentrated meaty flavor, often used as a base for other sauces. Making demi-glace from scratch takes some time; luckily it is available commercially in gourmet shops and on the Internet.

THE GUMBO POT

Anchoring the West Patio, the Gumbo Pot is your one-stop Cajun spot, serving delicious Big Easy eats steeped in tradition. Since opening in 1986, the Gumbo Pot has won critical praise and developed a die-hard following for their New Orleans–style specialties. The menu features traditional Southern Louisiana favorites like jambalaya, oyster po'boys, and, of course, gumbo.

Founding owner Charles Meyers was a musician who supported his tune-playing days by working at some of the most notable restaurants in New Orleans. When he relocated to Los Angeles, he was drawn to the bustling activity and street-scene ambiance of the Market, much like the vibe he loved in the French Quarter. He decided to put music on

the back burner and open the Gumbo Pot. He likens the complexity of Cajun cuisine to a folk song with its intricate layered story to tell. As his business grew, he hired soulful spirit Clinton Thompson, who began as a delivery driver in 1994 and worked his way up the ranks to general manager. Clinton embraced the caring, service-oriented atmosphere of the Gumbo Pot, as it fondly reminded him of his childhood, when he cooked stewed chicken with red beans and rice with his grandmother in Belize. Charles recognized Clinton's natural talent and passion for cooking, so began sharing his secret recipes and teaching him the underpinnings of running a restaurant. In 2005, Charles sold the Gumbo Pot to Clinton, knowing it would be in excellent hands and that the tastes and traditions of the Cajun kitchen would carry on. Today, Clinton revels in the therapeutic process of cooking and the feel-good factor of patrons enjoying his delicious dishes. A traditionalist at heart and the father of six, Clinton plans for the Gumbo Pot to be in his family for a long time.

Every February, the Market hosts the coolest Mardi Gras party this side of Bourbon Street. They offer outstanding Cajun bands, mask making, bead tossing, and a healthy supply of Dixie Beer. This is the busiest day of the year at the Gumbo Pot. Their New Orleans–style cuisine is always a delicious part of the celebration.

Seafood Gumbo with Cornbread Muffins

Without question, gumbo is the biggest seller at the Gumbo Pot. The Creole mainstay comes in two versions, milder seafood (brimming with shrimp and crab) and the spicier ya ya (fired up with andouille sausage). Making gumbo takes love and time. It's best to make it a day ahead; this will allow all the flavors to marry well. And don't forgo the secret ingredient: as they say in the bayou, if it ain't got okra, it ain't gumbo!

SERVES 6

½ cup canola oil

½ cup all-purpose flour

2 yellow onions, chopped

2 celery stalks, chopped

1 green bell pepper, seeded and chopped

6 garlic cloves, finely chopped

6 fresh thyme sprigs

4 bay leaves

1 teaspoon sea salt

1 teaspoon red pepper flakes

1 can (15 ounces) chopped tomatoes, with juice

2 quarts vegetable broth

2 pounds large shrimp, peeled with tails on

½ pound fresh lump crabmeat, picked over for cartilage and shell fragments

2 tablespoons filé powder (ground sassafras) (see Notes)

1 pound okra, fresh or frozen then thawed, cut into ¼-inch slices and roasted (see Notes)

3 cups cooked long-grain white rice

Chopped fresh flat-leaf parsley and green onions for garnish

Cornbread Muffins (page 133) for serving

Place a Dutch oven or other large, heavy-bottomed pot over medium heat and add the oil. When the oil gets hazy, sprinkle in the flour, a little at a time, and whisk constantly to prevent lumps. Cook and stir until the roux is smooth and thick and the color of peanut butter, about 10 minutes. Be very careful to keep the roux from scorching.

131

continued

Add the onions, celery, bell pepper, garlic, thyme, and bay leaves; season with the salt and red pepper flakes. Cook, stirring, until the vegetables are very soft, about 10 minutes. Pour in the tomatoes with their juice and the broth, stirring to combine. Bring the mixture to a boil, and then reduce the heat to medium-low. Gently simmer, uncovered, stirring occasionally, until the gumbo is dark and thick, 45 minutes to 1 hour.

Add the shrimp and crabmeat and simmer until the shrimp turn pink, 6 to 8 minutes; taste and adjust the seasoning if needed.

Dissolve the filé powder in ¼ cup of cold water and add directly to the pot. Continue to simmer for 5 minutes; do not let the gumbo boil after adding the filé. Remove from the heat and add the roasted okra, stirring to incorporate and heat through.

Ladle the gumbo into shallow soup bowls and pile a heaping spoonful or two of rice in the center of each serving. Garnish with a sprinkle of parsley and green onion. Serve hot, with the Cornbread Muffins.

Ingredient Notes—

Okra needs to be roasted a bit so it dries out and doesn't become slimy in the gumbo, which for some is a real turnoff. To do so, cut the okra into ¼-inch slices and arrange in a single layer on a baking pan. Roast in a preheated 375°F oven until firm to the touch, about 20 minutes.

Filé is the magic powder in Louisiana gumbo. Made of ground sassafras leaves, filé powder is used as a thickener but should only be stirred in at the end of cooking. Boiling filé will cause the gumbo to become stringy.

CORNBREAD MUFFINS

This moist and slightly spicy cornbread makes an excellent side for the Seafood Gumbo. If you prefer, bake in a 9-inch square baking pan and cut into 12 pieces.

MAKES 12 MUFFINS

1 cup yellow cornmeal	1 cup milk
1 cup all-purpose flour	2 large eggs
2 teaspoons baking powder	1 cup canned creamed corn
2 tablespoons sugar	1 cup shredded yellow Cheddar cheese
1 teaspoon salt	½ cup canned green chiles, drained

Preheat the oven to 400°F. Coat a standard 12-cup muffin tin with nonstick cooking spray.

In a large bowl, combine the cornmeal, flour, baking powder, sugar, and salt and stir to mix.

In another bowl, whisk together the milk, eggs, creamed corn, cheese, and chiles. Add the wet ingredients to the dry ingredients and stir just until incorporated.

Ladle the batter into the prepared pan, filling each cup two-thirds full. Tap the pan on the counter to settle the batter into the cups. Bake until golden and a toothpick inserted into the center of a muffin comes out clean, about 20 to 25 minutes. Serve hot or warm.

MAIN MEALS

133

HUNTINGTON MEATS & SAUSAGE

STALL
350

Dan Vance and Jim Cascone are the meat-loving owners of Huntington Meats & Sausage, servicing L.A.'s carnivore-savvy clientele with fine-quality products. After running the meat department in several high-end grocery stores, Dan Vance bought the place in 1988 from famous meat man John Tusquellas (see page 191), who had a renowned butcher shop in this spot for forty-five years. Dan changed the name and revamped the shop to include a spectrum of homemade sausages and deli items.

Dan came into the meat-cutting business as a thirteen-year-old when looking for a way to earn an allowance. He never thought that experience was the beginning of a lifelong love for the business. Jim Cascone, in his Chicago youth, was also a butcher's cleanup boy who went on to have a career in the grocery business. He partnered with Dan in 2002, and as it turned out, their expertise and personalities greatly complemented each other. Being a butcher is an art, and the harmonious back-and-forth banter that Dan and Jim have with each other and with their customers reflects their commitment to assessing each person's needs.

Jim has been making sausage his whole life. His delicious signature selections include meatloaf sausage, stuffed with pork, beef, and veal; Jamaican mango sausage, flavored with fresh mango and sweet-hot Cajun seasoning; and three-cheese Italian, rich with smoked mozzarella, Parmesan, and sharp provolone. Being a good Italian, Jim also knows his *salumi*. The service deli features an array of cured Italian meats, such as mortadella, sopressata, and pancetta, as well as specialty cheeses. All choices are cut, thick or thin, to the customer's personal preference. With products like these, alongside their exclusive high-quality Harris Ranch Prime Beef and chef's favorites like Wagyu beef and Korubuta pork, it's clear why once folks come to Huntington Meats, they become customers for life.

Hot and Sweet Italian Sausage and Peppers

At Huntington Meats & Sausage, butchers Dan and Jim hand twist nearly twenty varieties of sausage on the premises every day. All are produced in a natural casing with no MSG, sodium nitrates, or fillers. The premium roster ranges from Spanish chorizo to chicken apple sausage to lamb merguez. They even make a sausage-and-pepper sausage! These plump links of pork sausage are chock-full of savory flavor— some sweet, some hot, and all delicious. Serve this dish in bowls, over your favorite pasta, or on Italian sandwich rolls.

SERVES 4 TO 6

¼ cup extra-virgin olive oil

¾ pound hot Italian sausage, any variety

¾ pound sweet Italian sausage, any variety

4 garlic cloves, chopped

¼ teaspoon red pepper flakes

1 large red bell pepper, seeded and sliced

1 cubanelle pepper (mild Italian pepper), cored, seeded, and sliced

1 onion, sliced

2 bay leaves

1 teaspoon dried oregano

Kosher salt and freshly ground black pepper

¼ cup red wine vinegar

1 can (28 ounces) chopped tomatoes, preferably San Marzano, with juice

Pinch of sugar

½ cup chopped fresh basil

½ cup freshly grated Parmesan cheese, preferably Parmigiano-Reggiano

Place a large skillet over medium heat and coat with the oil. When the oil is hazy, add the sausages and brown on all sides, about 7 to 10 minutes. If necessary, work in batches to avoid overcrowding the pan. Using tongs, transfer the sausages to a paper towel–lined plate to drain.

Keeping the drippings in the pan, add the garlic and red pepper flakes.

Stir to coat in the oil for about 30 seconds; do not allow to burn. Add the peppers, onion, bay leaves, and oregano; season to taste with salt and pepper. Cook and stir until the vegetables have softened and cooked down, about 8 minutes.

Add the vinegar and stir to scrape up any browned bits from the bottom of the pan. Add the tomatoes with their juice and the sugar. Stir to combine and bring to a simmer.

Cut the sausages on the diagonal into 2-inch pieces. Return the sausage to the pan along with any accumulated juices and stir to incorporate. Gently simmer until the sauce has thickened, about 20 minutes.

Divide the sausage and peppers among individual plates and shower with the chopped basil. Serve immediately, passing the grated cheese at the table.

"I love the old-school atmosphere of Huntington Meats and the personal service that Jim and Dan provide. There are not many places anymore where you can talk to the actual butcher and tell them exactly what you want. Plus, of course, they have a hamburger mix named the 'Nancy Silverton Blend' that I highly recommend! It's freshly ground chuck with extra sirloin fat added for a real tasty, juicy burger. I also love the variety of sausages that I always get when I have a backyard barbecue. And very rarely do I walk by Huntington Meats and not pick up some of their excellent beef jerky. We eat it in the car, and by the time we get home, it's usually all gone."

— Nancy Silverton, co-owner of Pizzeria Mozza and Osteria Mozza

Nancy Silverton Burger Blend

Famed Los Angeles chef Nancy Silverton has been a faithful customer of Huntington Meats & Sausage for years. One day, Nancy told butcher and co-owner Jim Cascone that she was having a party and wanted to grill the ultimate burgers. She requested that Jim coarsely grind his prime chuck and add lots of ground sirloin fat to it so the burgers would be easier to form, fluffy, and really decadent tasting. Jim obliged, adding 10 percent of trimmed fat to the chuck, which brought the total fat content up to about 18 percent! The more meaty meat burgers were a huge hit at the party, and the buzz spread around the city's food scene. In fact, the *Los Angeles Times* food section printed a story on Nancy's pursuit of the perfect burger in 2005 and that day, Huntington Meats sold over four hundred pounds of their custom ground chunk! Food lovers swarmed the counter and asked if they too could get this deliciously fatty blend of beef. The requests kept coming in, and now Huntington Meats always keeps this concoction on hand, affectionately known as Nancy Silverton Burger Blend.

For the beef, ask the butcher to grind 2 pounds of prime chuck (10 percent fat) with 3 ounces of sirloin fat (the combination should have between 16 percent and 18 percent fat total).

SERVES 4

2 pounds ground chuck

Sea salt and freshly ground black pepper

Canola oil for brushing

8 slices Cheddar or Gruyère cheese

4 large sesame seed hamburger
buns, split

Crisp-cooked applewood-smoked bacon,
iceberg lettuce leaves, sliced tomatoes,
and red onion slices for serving

Ketchup, mayonnaise, and Dijon mustard
for serving

Huntington Meats New York deli pickles
for serving

Hand-form the ground beef into 4 huge burgers, being careful not to overwork the meat. Season both sides of the burgers with salt and pepper. Put a dimple in the center of each burger with your thumb, so the burgers' shape stay uniform as they cook and the tops don't dome.

Place a large grill pan on two burners over medium-high heat, prepare a fire in a charcoal grill, or preheat a gas grill to medium-high. Brush the hot grates with the oil to create a nonstick grilling surface. Grill the burgers for 8 minutes per side for medium; 6 minutes per side if you like your meat rare. The burgers should turn easily without sticking.

When the burgers are just about cooked, put a couple of slices of cheese on top of each and let it melt. Transfer the burgers to a platter so you have enough room to toast the buns.

Place the hamburger buns cut-side down on the grill pan or outdoor grill and toast for 1 minute. Serve the burgers immediately, either assembled or letting your guests build their own with the bacon, lettuce, tomato, onion, and condiments.

KADO

With Kado, the unique three-eateries-in-one Japanese restaurant situated at the corner where Farmers Market and the Grove intersect (*kado* means "corner" in Japanese), you don't have to go to Tokyo to have an authentic Japanese dining experience. Upon entering its inviting upstairs location, diners will be impressed by the unparalleled views outside and the hybrid culinary experience within. By combining fresher-than-fresh sushi served *keitan* style (on a conveyer belt), dishes from the teppan grill, and traditional fine dining, Kado offers something for everyone.

The *keitan*, or revolving conveyer belt sushi bar, is perfect for visitors wanting a bite and a break from shopping. Diners just pluck what they want from the moving sushi as it comes by on the belt, and the bill is calculated by the number of plates they have piled when they're finished. If guests are in the mood to settle in for flavorful food and engaging entertainment, Kado's Teppan Grill is the place. Here *teppan* chefs have an opportunity to show off their skills of agility as they slice and dice, stir, and season entrées with a sharp knife, a fork, and two metal spatulas right in front of diners' hungry eyes. While waiting to eat, they can marvel at the chefs' mastery on the *teppan* grill as they prepare Kobe filet mignon, black tiger shrimp, calamari steak, or lobster tail. And for a more mellow option, Kado also has a fine dining area with secluded booths. Delectable offerings on the menu include Rib Eye Miso with a Cabernet Reduction and Grilled Tuna served with Wasabi Mashed Potatoes. Whether it's for a light bite of sushi, the flare of the *teppan* grills, or a getaway for a formal dinner, the aura of Tokyo with its hustle and bustle, sophistication, and serenity is alive and well at Kado.

Diver Scallops with Blackberry Puree and Shiitake Risotto

This gorgeous dish has been a hit since Kado opened its doors. Meaty scallops perched on velvety risotto are a heavenly match. Scallops' strong supple flavor stands up beautifully to many big-flavored, sturdy elements, like sweet-tart black berries and smoky bacon fat.

SERVES 4

1 pint blackberries	1 cup olive oil
Juice of ½ lemon	16 large diver scallops (about 1½ pounds
2 tablespoons water	total weight)
1 tablespoon sugar	Sea salt and freshly ground black pepper
6 fresh basil leaves, torn by hand into	¼ cup bacon fat
small pieces	Shiitake Risotto (recipe follows) for serving
Needles of 2 fresh rosemary sprigs	Chopped fresh flat-leaf parsley for garnish
3 garlic cloves, smashed	

In a small pot over medium heat, combine the blackberries, lemon juice, water, and sugar. Stir gently until the berries break down and release their juices. Strain the blackberry puree through a fine-mesh strainer to remove the seeds. Set aside.

Combine the basil, rosemary, garlic, and oil in a food processor. Process until the oil is light green.

Season the scallops generously with salt and pepper and brush both sides with the herb oil. Place a large skillet over medium heat. Add the bacon fat, swirling the pan to coat. When the fat is hot, add 8 of the scallops, and sear for 2 minutes, without moving them around. When the bottoms of the scallops look nicely browned, turn them over and sear the other side for 1 minute.

Using tongs, carefully transfer the scallops to a platter lined with paper towels to blot some of the oil. Repeat to cook the remaining scallops.

To serve, mound 1 cup of the Shiitake Risotto in the center of each of 4 plates. Arrange 4 scallops on top. Dot the blackberry puree on the center of each scallop and drizzle around the plate. Garnish with a shower of chopped parsley.

SHIITAKE RISOTTO

Making risotto is often thought to be a time-intensive affair, but this recipe is ready in about 30 minutes. Specialty mushrooms like shiitakes are prized for their earthy flavor and meaty texture. If fresh shiitake mushrooms are not available, substitute cremini.

SERVES 4

2 tablespoons olive oil

1 shallot, minced

8 ounces shiitake mushrooms, stemmed, wiped clean, and sliced

2 tablespoons chopped fresh flat-leaf parsley, plus more for garnish

Sea salt and freshly ground black pepper

1 cup Japanese short-grain rice

½ cup dry white wine such as Pinot Grigio

4 cups low-sodium chicken broth, warm

1 cup heavy cream

2 tablespoons unsalted butter

½ cup freshly grated Parmesan cheese

Place a large, deep skillet over medium heat and coat with the oil. Add the shallot and cook and stir until soft, about 3 minutes. Add the mushrooms and the parsley and cook until the mushrooms release their liquid and are lightly browned, about 5 minutes. Season to taste with salt and pepper. Add the rice and stir until the grains are well-coated and opaque, 1 to 2 minutes. Taste and adjust the seasoning. Stir in the wine and cook for 1 minute to evaporate the alcohol.

Pour in 1 cup of the warm broth. Stir with a wooden spoon until the rice has absorbed all the liquid, then add another 1 cup. Keep stirring while adding the broth a cup at a time, allowing the rice to drink it in before adding more. You may not need all of the broth. Taste the risotto; it should be slightly firm but tender and creamy. Stir in the cream, butter, and cheese.

Japanese Rib Eye with Baby Bok Choy and Oyster Mushrooms

Marinades provide foundation flavors for many dishes. This recipe is based on a traditional Japanese marinade that pairs sake and soy. Sake helps "cook" the marinade into the steak, which is why it delivers such deep flavor. The melt-in-your-mouth texture is meant to be closer to a fine hunk of tuna than beef.

SERVES 4

Marinade	Vegetables
2½ cups low-sodium soy sauce	2 tablespoons vegetable oil
2 cups dry sake	1 shallot, minced
¼ cup vegetable oil	2 garlic cloves, minced
¼ cup chili oil	1 teaspoon peeled and chopped
1 tablespoon peeled and grated	fresh ginger
fresh ginger	4 heads baby bok choy, quartered
1 tablespoon grated garlic	lengthwise
1 tablespoon grated daikon (optional)	6 ounces oyster mushrooms, stemmed,
	wiped clean, and sliced
4 boneless rib-eye steaks (8 to	Kosher salt and freshly ground
10 ounces each)	black pepper
Vegetable oil for brushing	½ cup vegetable broth or water
Freshly ground black pepper	1 tablespoon soy sauce

To make the marinade: Combine all the ingredients in a large bowl and stir to mix well.

Lay the steaks in a baking dish and pour the marinade over them. Cover and refrigerate for at least 10 minutes but no longer than 25 minutes, or beef will become salty.

Remove the steaks from the marinade and pat dry with paper towels. Brush the steaks with the oil and season both sides generously with pepper; you should see the seasoning on the meat.

Place a large grill pan on two burners over medium-high heat, prepare a fire in a charcoal grill, or preheat a gas grill to medium-high. Lay the steaks on the hot grill and sear for 4 to 5 minutes on each side, rotating them halfway through cooking to create crisscross grill marks. Transfer the steaks to a cutting board and let rest for 10 minutes, so the juices can settle back into the meat.

To make the vegetables: Place a large skillet over medium-high heat and coat with the oil. When the oil is hazy, add the shallot, garlic, and ginger. Cook and stir for 1 minute to soften. Add the bok choy and mushrooms; season with salt and pepper. Cook and stir until the vegetables soften and begin to brown, about 4 minutes. Pour in the broth and soy sauce. Cook until the vegetables are tender and the liquid is almost totally evaporated, about 2 minutes longer.

Serve the steaks whole or carve on the diagonal into ½-inch slices. Arrange on individual plates with the vegetables on the side.

LA KOREA

STALL
510

America's education in Asian cuisine is advancing, and diners are ready to graduate to the next semester of Eastern flavors. Today, there is a ground swell of interest growing for Korean food. La Korea husband-and-wife owners Mimi and Michael Hong were ahead of the trend and excited to offer the delicacies of their homeland to Farmers Market customers. In fact, Mimi, an enthusiastic cook and entertainer, was so thrilled to be part of the community when they opened in 2003 that she prepared a feast for Farmers Market executives to introduce them to the tantalizing tastes of her country. Similar yet different enough from Chinese and Japanese food, Korean dishes balance and blend sweet, salty, bitter, hot, and sour elements. As a result, simple yet strong tangy flavors come together to create healthful combinations of fresh vegetables, rice, glass noodles, and tofu.

More and more people desire clean flavors and appreciate fast food where nothing is fried. One of La Korea's most requested dishes is *bibimbap*, a huge bowl of warm rice topped with sautéed and seasoned vegetables with a mildly spicy soy-based sauce. You can order tofu, chicken, pork, or beef to go on top. The ingredients are stirred together thoroughly just before eating. Korean barbecue dishes are also extremely popular; the *kalbi* comes with a choice of three side dishes such as glass noodles, seaweed salad, or Korean slaw.

The Hongs' philosophy is a straightforward one: They believe using the finest of ingredients in their home-style cooking makes all of the difference—it's authentic dishes made with love and with beautiful presentation. La Korea's enticing menu is reason enough for the interest in Korean fare to continue to thrive.

Kalbi (Marinated Short Ribs) with Korean Slaw

Kalbi **is the signature dish of Korean barbecue. These tender beef short ribs are bathed in a salty-sweet marinade and quickly grilled to sear in all the flavor. Like most Korean meals,** *kalbi* **is typically served with a wonderful assortment of side dishes.**

SERVES 4

1 large onion, quartered

6 garlic cloves, coarsely chopped

1 cup sugar

2 teaspoons ground black pepper

1 cup soy sauce

½ cup dry red wine such as Merlot

2 tablespoons sesame oil

4 pounds Korean-cut bone-in beef short ribs (see Note)

Vegetable oil for brushing

1 teaspoon toasted sesame seeds

Korean Slaw (recipe follows) for serving

Cooked white rice for serving

Put the onion and garlic in a food processor and pulse until finely chopped. Transfer the mixture to a large bowl. Add the sugar, pepper, soy sauce, wine, and sesame oil. Stir to combine and dissolve the sugar.

Put the ribs in a large plastic bag, pour in the marinade, squeeze out any air, and seal closed. Marinate in the refrigerator for at least 1 hour or up to overnight, turning the bag a couple of times.

Place a large grill pan on two burners over medium-high heat, prepare a fire in a charcoal grill, or preheat a gas grill to medium-high. (You can also use your oven broiler.)

Remove the ribs from the marinade. Brush the grill grates lightly with the oil. Place the ribs on the grill meaty-side down and cook, turning as needed, until well browned but still pink inside, about 5 minutes total. Set the ribs aside to rest for 5 minutes. Sprinkle with the sesame seeds. Serve with the Korean Slaw and white rice.

Ingredient Note—Short Ribs

Korean-style short ribs, also known as flanken or crosscut, are sliced crosswise across the bones instead of between the ribs. You end up with a strip of meat about 8 inches long that has 3 slivers of rib bones lining the bottom. This thin cut not only helps the meat absorb the marinade but also makes eating easier, particularly with chopsticks. Korean-style short ribs can be found at most butchers and Asian markets. If not available, butterfly the meat by slicing each rib lengthwise almost to the bone and opening it up like a book.

KOREAN SLAW

The delicious snap of Mimi's slaw is as tasty as it is healthful.

SERVES 4

¼ head red cabbage, cored and cut crosswise into shreds	3 tablespoons canola oil
	1 tablespoon sesame oil
1 head green cabbage, cored, quartered, and cut crosswise into shreds	1 cup white vinegar
	2 tablespoons sugar
1 carrot, grated	2 teaspoons salt

Soak the red cabbage in a bowl of cold water for 30 minutes to draw out some of the color so it doesn't bleed into the slaw. Drain, dry well, and put in a large bowl. Add the green cabbage and carrot; toss with your hands to combine. Drizzle in both oils, tossing well to coat the vegetables. Combine the vinegar, sugar, and salt in a bottle or jar and shake to blend well. Pour the vinegar mixture over the slaw and toss to combine.

MAGEE'S KITCHEN

STALL
625

When you eat at Magee's Kitchen, you're actually sinking your teeth into a direct descendent of the first Farmers Market restaurant. Without question, Phyllis Magee is the matriarch of the Market. Her mother-in-law, Blanche Magee, was the very first vendor to sell prepared food here in 1934. Blanche is credited with laying the Market's original water and electrical lines—no small task. After noticing customers sitting on fruit crates to eat, her son Paul (Phyllis's husband) was inspired to install tables and chairs, adding a key element to the atmosphere of the Market. As the tale goes, Blanche would drive past the corner of Third and Fairfax on her way home and see farmers parked in the vacant lot selling vegetables and fruit from their trucks. Phyllis jokes that Blanche was a nosy lady, and stopped to investigate what was going on. The farmers knew Blanche from downtown L.A.'s Grand Central Market, where she and her husband Ray already had a nut shop (see page 68) and the original Magee's Kitchen. Blanche took to visiting with the farmers and brought them ham and salads to snack on. Soon, their customers saw the ham sandwiches she made and started insisting that she sell to them, too. And with that, Magee's became the first nonfarmer tenant to establish roots at Third and Fairfax.

Phyllis Magee has carried on the legacy and still uses the same recipes Blanche developed for carrot and raisin salad, ground horseradish, and coleslaw. Everyone knows Phyllis and considers her the unofficial Market mentor. But she says her greatest joy is when longtime customers bring their babies in to see her because she knew *them* at that age. Blanche Magee lived to be 102—she died in 2000—and every chance she'd get, she'd have family bring her down to the Market to look over the business. Phyllis shares, "This place is our lives, and we have been here since the beginning and will continue to be here forever. Farmers Market is our home and has never let us down."

Magee's Roast Turkey, Parsley Potatoes, and Stewed Zucchini

Since the beginning, Magee's Kitchen has had the amazing ability to turn homey comfort food, which can be bland in the wrong hands, into something remarkable and tastefully simple. To keep up with the health-conscious times, Phyllis added roast turkey breast to the menu in 1985. She selects only the finest free-range birds for her discerning customers, and her supplier is none other than Puritan Poultry (see page 183).

SERVES 6 TO 8

1 whole bone-in turkey breast (6 to 7 pounds), preferably free-range

Kosher salt and freshly ground black pepper

¼ cup all-purpose flour

Parsley Potatoes (facing page) for serving

Stewed Zucchini (page 154) for serving

Preheat the oven to 350°F and remove the top rack so the turkey fits.

Rinse the turkey breast with cold water and pat dry with paper towels. Sprinkle the skin generously with salt and pepper. Put the turkey, breast-side up, in a large roasting pan. Cook until an instant-read thermometer inserted in the thickest part of the breast registers 160 to 165°F, about 2 hours. If the turkey begins to get too dark before it is cooked through, cover loosely with aluminum foil. Transfer the turkey to a cutting board and let rest for 15 minutes before carving, so the juices can settle back into the meat. In the meantime, make the gravy.

In a glass measuring cup or small bowl, combine the flour with ¼ cup cool water and stir to mix well. Add to the roasting pan and stir into the pan juices, scraping up any browned bits from the bottom of pan. Place the pan over high heat and bring to a boil, then reduce to medium-low and simmer until the gravy thickens slightly, about 3 minutes. Remove from heat and season to taste with salt and pepper.

Carve the turkey and serve with the gravy, potatoes, and zucchini.

PARSLEY POTATOES

Boiled potatoes are one of life's most satisfying simple pleasures. Brushed with butter and topped with fresh parsley, this recipe makes a terrific all-purpose side dish.

SERVES 4 TO 6

2½ pounds small red or white new potatoes, peeled

1 teaspoon kosher salt

¼ cup (½ stick) unsalted butter, melted

½ cup finely chopped fresh curly parsley

Put the potatoes in a large pot and add cold water to cover. Add the salt and bring to a boil over high heat, uncovered. Reduce the heat to medium and simmer until there is no resistance when a fork is inserted into the potatoes, about 30 minutes. Drain the potatoes well in a colander.

Spread the potatoes out in a shallow baking pan. Brush with the melted butter and sprinkle evenly with the parsley. The parsley potatoes can be held in a warm oven.

153

STEWED ZUCCHINI

This comforting dish is super simple to prepare and reminds folks of eating at grandma's house.

SERVES 4 TO 6

2 tablespoons corn oil

1 onion, chopped

½ teaspoon sugar

¼ teaspoon garlic powder

1 teaspoon kosher salt

¼ teaspoon freshly ground black pepper

1 can (28 ounces) diced tomatoes, with juice

½ teaspoon dried basil

8 to 10 small green zucchini, cut into 1-inch slices

Place a pot over medium-low heat and coat with the oil. When the oil is hazy, add the onion, sugar, garlic powder, ½ teaspoon of the salt, and the pepper. Cook slowly until the onion is soft but not browned, about 10 minutes. Carefully pour in the tomatoes with their juice and add the basil. Stir the sauce to combine the ingredients. Simmer gently, uncovered, stirring occasionally, for 30 minutes, to allow the flavors to marry.

Bring a large pot of water to a simmer. Add the zucchini and cover. Cook until tender, 3 to 4 minutes. Stir in the remaining ½ teaspoon salt, then drain. Arrange the zucchini on a platter and spoon the desired amount of tomato sauce on top.

"The hot corned beef platter at Magee's is my favorite in the city. I always get it with cabbage and boiled potatoes with a little bit of mustard and fresh horseradish on the side. The corned beef has the perfect amount of fat . . . just like I like it."

— Govind Armstrong, chef/co-owner of Table 8

MARCONDA'S MEATS

Butchers are a breed, and the family legacy at Marconda's Meats, at three generations strong, has one of the most robust histories at Farmers Market. Fred (Alfred) Marconda, who opened at the Market circa 1941, is the name behind the place. He learned the tasks of the trade when he was a kid back in Pennsylvania from his uncle Louis DeRosa, who operated a slaughterhouse. Louis's son, Dave, also worked with his father; he and cousin Fred were very close. Dave was in the air force and stationed in Los Angeles when World War II ended, and he joined Fred at this butcher shop. After years of working together, Dave DeRosa took over the business in 1977 when Fred retired and kept the family name of the butcher shop. Dave has continued to champion their philosophy: that people want personal service, the ability to choose exactly what they want, and to be greeted with a friendly salutation. Rare pampering like eye contact and expert cooking advice keeps customers coming back.

To work at Marconda's, candidates must go through rigorous basic training. Lesson One is learning everything in the meat case. The selection is amazing: a wide range of steaks and chops, roasts butchered to your liking, beef and lamb dry-aged on site, ground beef, and pork. Lesson Two is identifying what cooking method is ideal for which cut and type. Lesson Three is learning the art of butchering with little waste and pristine cuts. Everything at Marconda's is immaculately clean and white, including the butcher's aprons.

Dave, recognizable by his white hair and mustache, still works when he is here, which he says keeps him happy, healthy, and sharp. He is pleased that this landmark establishment is alive and well and remains in family hands. To Dave and his son, Lou, who followed in the family footsteps and opened Puritan Poultry (see page 183), meat will always be the heart and soul of the matter.

Meatloaf Deluxe

While some may be afraid to admit it, it seems like everyone loves meatloaf; there is no denying it is the king of comfort food. At Marconda's, meatloaf is both a family and a customer favorite. In the old days, Fred used to simply sell the meat and give his recipe to go with it. Today, Dave DeRosa prepares his cousin's meatloaf in disposable loaf pans for their customers' convenience.

SERVES 6 TO 8

2 pounds extra-lean ground beef

1 pound mild ground pork sausage

½ cup plain dried bread crumbs

2 tablespoons chopped onion

2 tablespoons chopped celery

1 tablespoon chopped fresh flat-leaf parsley

2 tablespoons seasoning salt

2 large eggs

½ cup ketchup, plus more for brushing

Preheat the oven to 350°F.

In a large bowl, combine the ground beef and pork sausage with the bread crumbs, onion, celery, parsley, seasoning salt, eggs, and the ½ cup ketchup. This is where you get your hands dirty! Mix by hand until just blended; take care not to overmix.

Fill a 9-by-5-inch loaf pan with the meat mixture and flatten the top with a spatula. Brush a thin layer of ketchup on top; this holds in the juices. Place the pan on a baking pan to prevent the drippings from burning on the bottom of the oven. Bake the meatloaf, uncovered, until it pulls away from the sides of the pan, about 1 hour and 45 minutes. Let cool for 10 minutes. Cut into slices and serve.

Roasted Leg of Lamb with Garlic and Rosemary

Dry-aging is an investment in time and money that few butchers are willing to make. But at Marconda's Meats, they wouldn't have it any other way. All-natural Colorado lamb is meticulously aged in a cooler on the premises for twenty-one days. The process concentrates the natural flavor through evaporation and makes the lamb extra-tender. Bone-in leg of lamb has marvelous flavor and is a traditional roast for festive family gatherings. If you can't get to Marconda's, have your butcher trim away the white skin that covers the lamb (also called fell) as well as the excess fat.

SERVES 6 TO 8

1 bone-in leg of lamb (about 6 pounds)	Juice of 2 lemons
6 garlic cloves, minced	¼ cup olive oil
2 tablespoons finely chopped fresh rosemary	1 tablespoon kosher salt
	1 teaspoon freshly ground black pepper

Preheat the oven to 400°F.

Put the lamb in a large roasting pan and pat dry with paper towels.

In a small bowl, combine the garlic, rosemary, lemon juice, oil, salt, and pepper. Mix well to form a paste. Using your hands, rub the paste all over the lamb.

Place the lamb in the oven and roast for 30 minutes. Reduce the oven temperature to 350°F and continue to cook for about 1 hour longer for medium-rare, or until a meat thermometer inserted into the center of the roast registers about 135°F (be careful that the thermometer does not touch the bone).

Remove the lamb to a cutting board and let rest for 10 minutes, so the juices can settle back into the meat (the internal temperature will continue to rise 5 to 10 degrees). Carve and serve.

A leg of lamb is one of the simplest roasts to carve. There are no complicated techniques involved, and the only tools required are a sharp knife and a cutting board. Hold the leg bone securely with a clean kitchen towel and lift it up slightly so the leg is tilted. Slice the rounded side of the meat into thin pieces until you hit the bone. Turn the leg over so it sits steady on the board and carve the other side in the same manner. Cutting should always be across the grain of the meat, which radiates outward from the bone; this produces more tender slices.

MARMALADE CAFÉ

Breakfast anyone? Brunch, lunch, or dinner? All types of meals with a classic California twist are available at Marmalade Cafe, opened in 2002 and located just on the outskirts of the Market Plaza. Owners Bobby, Bonnie, and Selwyn learned the restaurant biz from working at their family-owned old Los Angeles favorite Bob Burns. With all that experience between them, they opened their first Marmalade Café in 1990 in Santa Monica to rave reviews. The team began as a catering company before they developed their concept for a versatile and dynamic café, and their restaurateuring talents have now spread their enterprise throughout the Southland, in locations that they feel attract customers who appreciate their eclectic cuisine. To them, the true spirit of Los Angeles is wonderfully apparent in the unique historical setting of Farmers Market. They have fond childhood memories here and are thrilled to have Marmalade be a part of a new generation of merchants.

Adorned with funky antiques and artifacts from all over the United States, the attractive décor is in keeping with Marmalade's appealing cuisine. In this cafe, the history of the first Bob Burns Restaurant lives on through the chandeliers that now hang in the dining room. Try the tortilla scramble for breakfast or any one of the flavorful soups, salads, or sandwiches for lunch. For dinner, dig into one of their single-serving pizzas, quesadillas, or diversely prepared chicken breast, fresh fish, or meat specialties. And be sure to leave room for one of their delectable desserts. No matter what the time of day or the menu choice, patrons will leave Marmalade Café happy and full.

Linguine di Mare

This vibrant dish features the "fruits of the sea"—shrimp, calamari, and scallops—tossed with linguine in a spicy marinara sauce. It's one of the most requested entrees at Marmalade; the seafood fills the restaurant with its intoxicating aroma.

SERVES 4

1½ pounds linguine

Extra-virgin olive oil for drizzling, plus 2 tablespoons

16 large shrimp (about 1 pound), peeled with tails on

16 bay scallops (about 1 pound)

Sea salt and freshly ground black pepper

4 garlic cloves, thinly sliced

½ teaspoon red pepper flakes

½ teaspoon saffron threads

1 plum (Roma) tomato, seeded and chopped

4 fresh basil leaves, cut into ribbons, plus more for garnish

½ cup dry white wine such as Sauvignon Blanc

2 cups marinara sauce

½ cup heavy cream

¾ pound calamari, cleaned and cut into rings

2 tablespoons unsalted butter

Bring a large pot of well-salted water to boil. Add the linguine and return to a boil. Cook, stirring occasionally, until just tender but still firm to the bite (al dente), about 8 minutes. Drain in a colander and drizzle with a little oil to keep it from sticking.

Place a large skillet over medium-high heat and coat with the 2 tablespoons olive oil. When the oil is hazy, add the shrimp and scallops and toss just until opaque, about 1 minute. Season to taste with salt and pepper. Add the garlic, red pepper flakes, saffron, chopped tomato, and basil; toss until fragrant, about 1 minute. Pour in the wine and cook until it is almost totally evaporated.

Add the marinara and cream; bring to a boil and cook until slightly reduced, about 2 minutes. Add the calamari and cook until tender, 1 to 2 minutes. Add the pasta and toss to coat. Toss with the butter. Divide among 4 bowls, shower with basil ribbons, and serve immediately.

MONSIEUR MARCEL PAIN, VIN, ET FROMAGE

STALLS 144 & 236

Fresh crusty bread, deep or delicate wine, and provocative, even stinky, cheese are perfect French fare. Provençal perfection in a charming bistro setting awaits patrons at Monsieur Marcel Pain, Vin, et Fromage, located just across from the majestic Monsieur Marcel Gourmet Market (see page 82). Stephane Strouk, owner of both places, knew right away that he wanted to bring unpretentious French food to Los Angeles. He felt a connection with the alfresco atmosphere of Farmers Market and its resemblance to European open-air markets. The Market also stirs happy memories for Stephane of working with his mother at her corner crêpe stand on the streets of Paris. Stephane often drew a crowd and stopped traffic as he tossed crêpes with flair.

Stephane came to Los Angeles on vacation when he was twenty-three years old, met his wife-to-be, fell in love, and moved to the city for good in 1993. Starting off with what he knew best, he founded the French Crêpe Company (see page 59). He sold that, but expanded at the same time to create Monsieur Marcel Gourmet Market. Opening a restaurant to feature his own excellent imports was a natural progression, and he established Pain, Vin, et Fromage in 2002. The menu lists a little bit of everything *français* with a lot of flavor and panache. Guests can sit at the comfortable, horseshoe-shaped wooden wine bar while nibbling on picholine olives and sipping a chilled rosé or a full-bodied Burgundy, then finish their meal at one of the cozy candlelit tables. Locals and visitors alike find their way to this little corner jewel of Provence. Stephane appreciates every bit of his success and is passing on his love for all things French to his young daughter by teaching her to cook, particularly the traffic-stopping art of crêpe making.

Fondue Savoyarde

Gourmet grocery and restaurant owner Stephane Strouk takes his cheese seriously. The maestro spent two years perfecting his fondue, which maintains a velvet consistency, sans the addition of any added starch. His secret? French Dijon mustard.

SERVES 6 TO 8

1 garlic clove, crushed

1½ cups Apremont (Lacquère grape wine)

¼ cup kirsch (cherry brandy), plus more for finishing the pot (optional)

¾ pound Gruyère de Comté cheese, coarsely grated

¾ pound Gruyère de Beaufort cheese, coarsely grated

¾ pound Appenzeller cheese, coarsely grated

¾ pound Morbier cheese, coarsely grated

¼ pound Roquefort cheese

1 tablespoon Dijon mustard

Pinch of freshly grated nutmeg

Kosher salt and freshly ground white pepper

3 baguettes, cut into bite-size pieces

1 large egg

Rub the inside of a fondue pot or heavy pot with the garlic clove. Leave the garlic in the pot. Pour in the Apremont and kirsch and bring to a boil over medium heat on the stove top. Gradually incorporate the grated Gruyère de Comté, Gruyère de Beaufort, Appenzeller, and Morbier cheeses, stirring constantly in a figure-8 pattern with a wooden spoon.

When the cheeses are entirely melted, add the Roquefort, mustard, and nutmeg. Season to taste with salt and pepper. Stir to mix, taking care not to let the fondue boil.

To serve, set the fondue pot on the table over a fondue burner and let diners spear pieces of bread with fondue forks and plunge them into the fondue. Remember to stir the fondue in a figure-8 pattern even when dipping your fork, to keep it from separating or sticking to the bottom.

When the fondue is nearly finished, clean up the pot with this edible trick: Put in a few pieces of bread, add the egg and a good portion of kirsch, if desired, and place over high heat back on the stove top. Stir with a wooden spoon until the mixture thickens; this will help get the cheese off the pot. Remove from the heat when the mixture is lightly brown, and let diners pick out the pieces of bread with their fondue forks.

Variations—Mushrooms and Ham

Add dried mushrooms, such as porcini or morels, along with the wine when you start. Roll your bread in a strip of ham or prosciutto before plunging your fork into the fondue, or serve a spread of fine cold cuts side-by-side with the fondue.

167

Steak Frites
with Cognac-Mushroom Sauce

Steak frites, French foodese for steak and fries, is a classic wine-friendly union enjoyed at every convivial Paris bistro. Bistros in France are well-loved eateries, known for the simple and hearty fare they serve. Monsieur Marcel Pain, Vin, et Fromage is that little neighborhood restaurant where you'll find simplicity, in abundance. Should you go French in Farmers Market? *Oui*!

SERVES 4

Sauce	Steak
2 tablespoons unsalted butter	4 New York strip steaks (about 8 ounces each)
1 shallot, minced	
2 garlic cloves, minced	Fine sea salt and freshly ground black pepper
8 ounces assorted mushrooms such as cremini, oyster, and chanterelle, wiped clean and sliced	1 tablespoon extra-virgin olive oil
Fine sea salt and freshly ground black pepper	**Frites (See Note)**
¼ cup Cognac or brandy	Canola or other vegetable oil for frying
1 cup low-sodium beef broth	4 large russet potatoes, peeled
½ cup heavy cream	1 teaspoon herbes de Provence
2 tablespoons finely chopped fresh flat-leaf parsley	Fine sea salt and freshly ground black pepper

168

To make the sauce: Melt the butter in a large skillet over medium-high heat. Add the shallot and garlic and cook, stirring often, until beginning to soften, about 1 minute. Add the mushrooms and season with salt and pepper to taste. Cook and stir until the mushrooms release their liquid and are lightly browned, about 5 minutes. Pour in the Cognac and stir, scraping up any browned bits from the bottom of the pan. Pour in the broth and cook until the liquid is reduced by half. Stir in the cream and simmer until the sauce is slightly thickened and coats the back of a spoon, about 2 minutes. Sprinkle with the parsley. Keep the sauce warm.

To make the steaks: Pat the steaks dry with paper towels and sprinkle all sides with a generous amount of salt and pepper—you should see the seasoning on the meat. Place a large skillet over medium-high heat, coat with the oil, and just when it begins to smoke, lay the steaks in the hot pan. Brown on all sides until a crust forms and the meat is well seared, about 7 minutes total for medium-rare. Remove the steaks to a warm platter to rest while you make the *frites*.

To make the *frites*: Pour the oil into a countertop deep fryer or deep heavy-bottomed pot to a depth of about 3 inches and heat to 350°F over medium-high heat. While the oil is heating, cut the potatoes into uniform ¼-inch sticks; use a knife, mandoline, or French fry cutter. Dry the potato shoestrings thoroughly with paper towels.

Fry the potatoes in batches so the oil temperature does not drop. Par-cook the *frites* for 3 minutes; the potatoes should not be crisp or fully cooked at this point, just a bit limp. Remove the *frites* with a long-handled metal strainer or skimmer and transfer to several layers of paper towel to drain. (This step may be done several hours before you need to finish cooking the *frites*.)

Raise the heat to bring the oil temperature to 375°F. Return the par-cooked potatoes to the oil in batches and fry them a second time until golden and crispy, about 2 minutes. Remove the potatoes from the oil to clean paper towels to drain. Season with the herbes de Provence and salt and pepper to taste while they are still hot.

To serve, arrange the steaks on individual plates. Drizzle the mushroom sauce over and pile the frites on the side. Serve immediately.

Ingredient Note—Frites

The key to perfect pommes frites is double frying. The first fry at a lower temperature gives the inside of the potato time to cook before the outside browns. The second fry at a higher temperature ensures crispness.

PAMPAS GRILL

STALL
618

Brazil is a simmering blend of samba, sand, and sensational food. Nobody has ever confused Los Angeles with Rio de Janeiro, but Brazilian-born Francisco Carvalho is hoping to create some doubt, aiming to bring a taste of his homeland to the corner of Third and Fairfax; Pampas is the grill from Ipanema. Francisco, who also owns Phil's Deli & Grill (see page 38), launched the *churrascaria* in 2001. *Churrasco*, the Brazilian word for "barbecue," originated centuries ago in the *pampas*, or prairie ranchlands, of southern Brazil. The fertile grassy plains of the *pampas* were the perfect land for grazing cattle. Brazilian cowboys, called *gauchos*, herded these cattle and created a new way of cooking. Distinctly a South American–style rotisserie, the cowboys speared big pieces of meat and roasted them over charcoal.

It seems fitting that Francisco would pay homage to the gauchos of past generations and name his *churrascaria* Pampas Grill. In the center of the restaurant, you'll see a large mesquite barbecue, where the finest cuts of meat are simply prepared and spit-roasted to juicy perfection. Just like they do in Brazil, Pampas Grill features buffet-style dining, where the food is priced by the pound. In Brazil, *comida a kilo*—literally, "food by the kilo"—restaurants are very common. Customers select dishes they want as they walk along and pay by weight at the end. Francisco points out that this way of eating is becoming very popular in L.A. because it gives guests the freedom to choose what they want and how much of it. The concept is clearly working, as Pampas Grill often has a line of hungry visitors that snake out through Gate 2. In addition to the custom-carved meat, the self-serve hot and cold buffet contains a bountiful selection of vegetarian sides, such as hearts of palm salad, fried plantains, black beans, braised collard greens, and other authentic Brazilian delights. When you come to Pampas Grill, you do not have to know the language, but you do need a healthy appetite.

Churrasco Picanha
with Fried Sweet Plantains
and Hearts of Palm Salad

Churrasco is typically made from *picanha*—an unadorned sirloin cut of beef. Seasoned simply with rock salt, the salt keeps the meat moist while it cooks without making it taste overly salty. In traditional *churrascarias*, all of the meat is roasted on 2-foot-long metal skewers and turned either by hand or with a rotisserie. If you can't get your hands on the extra-large skewers, as an alternative, you can still enjoy the same delicious flavor at home by simply rubbing the steaks with rock salt and grilling directly.

Churrasco is much more than a way of cooking in Brazil—it's a way of life. In most of the country, homemade *churrasco* is a typical weekend event, where it is enjoyed outdoors with beer, music, and watching soccer games on TV with friends. While Pampas Grill is a true carnivore's delight, one of its big surprises is the gigantic buffet. Fried Sweet Plantains and Hearts of Palm Salad are classic vegetable accompaniments to *picanha*.

SERVES 4

2 pounds picanha (top sirloin cap; see Note), untrimmed

½ cup rock salt

Fried Sweet Plantains (page 174) for serving

Hearts of Palm Salad (page 175) for serving

Prepare a fire in a charcoal grill, adding mesquite charcoal, if desired.

Divide the beef into 4 big pieces, making sure to cut across the grain. Sprinkle both sides of the steaks generously with the rock salt.

You can use skewers (the 2-foot-long traditional rotisserie skewer works well for all 4 pieces, or use 2 or more smaller skewers) or just cook the meat pieces unskewered. If using a skewer, thread it through the top and bottom of the meat to form a neat round chunk so you end up with a band of fat on the outside. This can be tricky, so take care not to skewer your hand, too.

continued

Put the meat on the grill over high heat and cook for 8 minutes. As it cooks, the fat will begin to melt away, marinating the meat, and the remaining fat will become crispy. Turn and cook the other side until nicely browned, about 7 minutes longer for medium-rare.

Once the meat is cooked to your liking, transfer to a platter to rest for 5 minutes. Brush off the excess salt and slice against the grain. Serve with the Fried Sweet Plantains and Hearts of Palm Salad.

Ingredient Note—Top Sirloin Cap

In the *churrasco* tradition, *gauchos*, the famed Brazilian cowboys, barbecue meat on long, swordlike skewers over an open-fire pit. Pampas Grill's signature cut, *picanha*, is an irresistible portion from the choicest part of the top sirloin called the "cap" (it is also known as coulotte steak or rump cover). There's one side that is mostly a large slab of fat, which drips down as it cooks over the open flame to flavor the meat. Authentically seasoned only with rock salt, the *picanha* cut is what creates such a distinct flavor. In Brazil, this unique cut is considered to be the best; it has the most marbling of the whole lean top sirloin, making it flavorful, juicy, and tender. You can find *picanha* in most Latin markets, or in any good butcher shop— just ask for the cap of the top sirloin.

FRIED SWEET PLANTAINS

Plantains are a staple in many Latin America countries, including Brazil. The sweet taste of the ripe plantain combined with the charred flavor of the beef makes for a surprisingly savory combination. If you have never tried plantains, this is a great way to begin, and if you have, you will absolutely love this dish.

SERVES 4

2 ripe yellow to black plantains

¼ teaspoon ground cinnamon

½ cup vegetable oil

Cut off the ends of each plantain and discard. Cut each plantain into 3 or 4 chunks. With a paring knife, make shallow slits lengthwise along the seams of the skin and peel off in sections. Cut the plantain pieces in half lengthwise.

Place a large skillet over medium-low heat and add the oil (ripe plantains have a high sugar content and will burn if the heat is too high). When the oil is hazy, carefully add the plantains and fry until golden on both sides, turning as needed, about 5 minutes. Sprinkle with the cinnamon. Remove to a plate lined with paper towels to drain. Serve immediately.

HEARTS OF PALM SALAD

Hearts of palm is the national ingredient of Brazil. At Pampas Grill, this delicate vegetable is used in a refreshing salad, where the light-crisp taste has a starring role.

SERVES 4

1 can (14 ounces) hearts of palm, drained, rinsed, and sliced (see Note)

1 pint cherry tomatoes

1 cucumber, quartered and sliced in chunks

1 garlic clove, minced

2 tablespoons finely chopped fresh flat-leaf parsley

Juice of 1 lime

¼ cup extra-virgin olive oil

Kosher salt and freshly ground black pepper

In a large bowl, combine the hearts of palm with the tomatoes, cucumber, garlic, and parsley. Add the lime juice and oil, and season with salt and pepper to taste. Toss the salad gently with your hands and serve.

Ingredient Note—Hearts of Palm

Hearts of palm are literally just that: the inner portion of the stems of palm trees. The ivory-colored cylinders are firm and smooth and the flavor is reminiscent of an artichoke heart. Canned hearts of palm are widely available.

Bacalhau (Portuguese Cod Fish)

Brazilian cooking spans a unique mix of a cultures and cuisines. This huge country is a tasty melting pot thanks to influences from the Native Americans, Europeans, and most notably, the Portuguese and Africans, who left a legacy of dishes. *Bacalhau*, dried salt cod, is a staple in the Brazilian kitchen. Introduced by the Portuguese, it finds its way into appetizers, soups, main courses, and savory puddings. This traditional baked casserole of salt cod, potatoes, onions, and olives is a regional favorite and loved by everyone. Note that you need to soak the cod a day ahead of time.

SERVES 4 TO 6

2 pounds dry salt cod (see Note)

½ cup olive oil, plus more for greasing

2 large onions, sliced

1 red bell pepper, seeded and sliced

1 green bell pepper, seeded and sliced

1 yellow bell pepper, seeded and sliced

2 garlic cloves, minced

Sea salt and freshly ground black pepper

2 pounds new potatoes, cut into slices ¼-inch thick

8 black olives, sliced, for garnish

2 tablespoons finely chopped fresh flat-leaf parsley for garnish

Starting 1 day ahead, soak the dried cod in cold water for 12 to 24 hours, changing the water several times to remove the majority of the salt. Drain the cod, rinse, and put it in a large pot. Add enough water to cover by 1 inch. Bring to a simmer over medium-low heat and cook gently until the cod is tender and pliable, about 15 minutes. Drain and rinse well, then flake the cod into a bowl with your hands, removing any little bits of skin and bone. Set aside.

Preheat the oven to 350°F.

Place a large skillet over medium heat and coat with ¼ cup of the oil. When the oil is hazy, add the onions, bell peppers, and garlic; season to taste with salt and pepper. Cook and stir until the vegetables soften and start to color, about 5 minutes.

Grease a medium casserole dish with a little oil. Arrange half of the potato slices over the bottom of the prepared dish, overlapping them slightly. Scatter half of the salt cod over the potatoes and spread half of the pepper mixture on top. Repeat the layers in the same order. Drizzle the entire pan with the remaining ¼ cup of oil. Bake until the top is golden, 30 to 40 minutes. Garnish with the olives and parsley and serve directly from the dish.

Ingredient Note—Dried Salt Cod

Preserving cod in salt, which removes the moisture, makes the fish firm and chewy. Salt cod is very popular in Brazil, Portugal, Italy, and Spain, although the cod itself generally comes from Norway. It must be reconstituted and soaked in several changes of water before using. It can usually be found in the seafood section of most grocery stores or at Latin American markets.

PEKING KITCHEN

STALL
508

When enjoying a Chinese meal from Peking Kitchen, patrons should know that behind the scenes, there is a delicious love story of fate and fried rice. Husband-and-wife team Tony and Annie Zou both grew up in the same town outside of Hong Kong and arrived in Los Angeles around the same time in the mid-1980s, though they never met—at least not yet. To augment his living expenses while a struggling student, Tony went to work as a dishwasher for his Aunty Betty, who had opened Peking Kitchen at the Market in the 1970s. At the time, her son was meant to be fixed up with a pretty Chinese girl named Annie, but he wasn't ready to settle down, so he passed on the matchmaking. Cousin Tony jumped in and proclaimed that he was keen to court this lovely young lady and get married. But because Tony was a poor student and a dishwasher, the matchmaker deemed him an unfit suitor. He continued to study hard at school and forgot about the girl when he fell in love with a beautiful classmate. Six months later at their wedding, the family friend who thought Tony wasn't good enough for Annie recognized him as the groom and exclaimed, "Annie, you're marrying the poor dishwasher?!" Tony and Annie never knew they were almost set up until their wedding day. Tony is convinced that they were destined to be together.

Aunty Betty groomed Tony and his bride to take over the Peking Kitchen when she retired in 1989. Annie, who has always enjoyed cooking and catering, prepares the food in back while Tony chats up the customers out front. They have an obvious yin-and-yang unity working together. Tony takes pride in his story of pursuing the American dream. He arrived here to learn, to work hard, and to succeed. He did all of that—and found the woman of his dreams! Tony jokes that while he still is washing dishes, at least now he owns the plates.

Black Pepper Chicken with Vegetable Fried Rice

Some like it hot! At Peking Kitchen, fiery foods like Black Pepper Chicken are a prime example of their sizzling Szechuan cuisine. The menu celebrates Chinese home-style cooking, meaning the dishes are quicker and easier to make, with less oil than those you commonly find in many Chinese restaurants. This is one of those places that proves the restaurant-goers theory that if people are standing at the counter waiting for the food, there must be a good reason.

SERVES 4

1 pound skinless, boneless chicken, white and dark meat, cut into strips

3 tablespoons vegetable oil

Kosher salt and freshly ground black pepper

3 teaspoons cornstarch

1 teaspoon finely ground Szechuan peppercorns or black peppercorns (see Note)

1 onion, cut into chunks

2 celery stalks, cut on the diagonal into 1-inch pieces

2 carrots, cut on the diagonal into 1-inch pieces

¼ pound green beans, trimmed and halved

¼ cup low-sodium chicken broth or water

2 tablespoons soy sauce

1 teaspoon sugar

Vegetable Fried Rice (page 182) for serving

Put the chicken in a bowl and coat with 1 tablespoon of the oil. Season the chicken with salt and black pepper and sprinkle with 1 teaspoon of the cornstarch. Toss to coat.

Coat a wok or large skillet with 1 tablespoon of the oil and place over high heat. When the oil is just about smoking, add the chicken to the pan and stir-fry until lightly browned and crispy, about 3 minutes. Transfer the chicken to a platter.

Add the remaining 1 tablespoon oil and the Szechuan pepper to the wok. Stir for about 10 seconds to allow the pepper to infuse the oil. Add the onion, tossing for a minute to soften. Add the celery, carrots, and green beans. Stir-fry until tender but not mushy, about 2 minutes.

In a small bowl, combine the broth, soy sauce, sugar, and remaining 2 teaspoons cornstarch and stir until the sugar and cornstarch are dissolved. Pour the soy sauce mixture into the wok and cook until the sauce has thickened, about 1 minute. Return the chicken to the pan and toss quickly until the sauce has coated the chicken and vegetables. Add more water to thin the sauce, if necessary. Serve immediately, with the Vegetable Fried Rice.

Ingredient Note—Szechuan Peppercorns

Hailing from China, Szechuan pepper is actually not a peppercorn at all but a berry from the prickly ash shrub. The flavor is lemony and has a pronounced woody aroma. Szechuan peppercorns can be purchased in Asian markets and the specialty spice section of many large supermarkets. You may substitute black peppercorns if desired. (A great tip to intensify black pepper's pungent flavor is to toast the peppercorns in a dry skillet over medium heat, shaking the pan so they don't burn. This releases the aromatic oils and makes the pepper a bit more fiery and full flavored. Let the peppercorns cool before filling your pepper grinder or spice mill.)

MAIN MEALS

VEGETABLE FRIED RICE

This is a great recipe to use day-old steamed rice from Chinese take-out. The rice dries out a bit in the fridge, and the grains stay separate when you fry in the wok.

SERVES 4

2 tablespoons vegetable oil

2 green onions, white and green parts, thinly sliced

2 garlic cloves, minced

1 teaspoon peeled and grated fresh ginger

2 large eggs, lightly beaten

1 pint cooked long-grain white rice

1 cup thawed frozen peas and carrots

3 tablespoons soy sauce

Kosher salt and freshly ground black pepper

Fresh cilantro for garnish

Place a wok or large skillet over medium-high heat and coat with the oil. When the oil is hazy, add the green onions, garlic, and ginger and stir-fry until fragrant, about 1 minute. Move the ingredients to the side of the pan and pour the eggs into the center. Scramble the eggs lightly, just until set but not brown. Fold in the rice and toss everything together to combine well, breaking up any rice clumps with the back of a spatula.

Add the peas and carrots to the pan and moisten with the soy sauce. Toss the ingredients together to heat through and season to taste with salt and pepper. Spoon the fried rice onto a serving platter, garnish with the cilantro, and serve.

PURITAN POULTRY

Which came first, the chicken or the egg? When shopping at Puritan Poultry, patrons don't have to decide, since the best of both are sold. When father-and-son butchers Dave and Lou DeRosa took over Puritan Poultry in 1990, they knew times were changing and the culinary trend was moving toward lean meats like poultry. It was a natural progression to complement their already successful meat shop (see page 155). Puritan carries not only free-range chicken, plump turkeys, and super-fresh jumbo eggs but also exotic fowl like Cornish hens, squab, and quail, whole birds or specific cuts boned and skinned into picture-perfect pieces.

The DeRosa family has a loyal fan base, some going back three and four generations, as well as a younger crowd who are conscious about what they eat. Lou appreciates that this new wave of inquisitive cooks asks questions and are keen to learn. There is a face and a name behind this hands-on business: besides the butchers, the familiar face of manager Rito Marquez is there, happy to help, six days a week. This isn't an easy trade to master. The hours are long, the work is hard, and rarely is there a vacation. As Lou always says, "In the meat business, you never get rich, but you never go hungry." It is a good thing that deep down Lou wanted to be a butcher just like his old man, Dave. At one point in the 1980s, to try something different, Lou worked in the world of furniture with his brother-in-law, but couldn't escape his destiny and proved extremely handy with a knife. Say hi to Lou next time you're at Marconda's Meats or Puritan Poultry.

MAIN MEALS

183

Stuffed Breast of Chicken

At Puritan Poultry, you'll find not only the best birds in town but also freshly prepared take-home meals that are ready to pop in the oven. The butchers even supply the disposable baking pan! The ready-made stuffed chicken breasts are one of the great conveniences for time-pressed customers who crave a home-style meal from scratch. If you can't get to the Market to pick some up, give their recipe a try at home.

SERVES 4

Stuffing

2 cups fresh bread crumbs

½ cup cooked wild rice pilaf

¼ cup finely chopped small onion

2 tablespoons finely chopped celery

2 tablespoons finely chopped green bell
    pepper

2 tablespoons finely chopped red bell
    pepper

2 teaspoons poultry seasoning

Juice of ½ lemon

½ to ¾ cup low-sodium chicken broth

4 skin-on boneless chicken breasts (about
    2 pounds total)

2 tablespoons sweet paprika

1 tablespoon granulated garlic

1 tablespoon kosher salt

1 teaspoon freshly ground black pepper

½ teaspoon cayenne pepper

Pinch of sugar

To make the stuffing: Combine the bread crumbs, cooked pilaf, onion, celery, bell peppers, and poultry seasoning in a bowl. Moisten the filling with the lemon juice and broth, mixing until the ingredients are evenly incorporated and the stuffing holds together when pressed.

Put the chicken breasts, skin-side up, on a cutting board. Using a sharp knife, carefully cut a horizontal slit about half of the way through each chicken breast to make a pocket. Open the pockets up with your fingers and fill completely with the stuffing. Fold the edges together to cover the opening or secure with toothpicks.

Preheat the oven to 350°F.

Place the stuffed chicken breasts skin-side up in a small baking pan, making sure the skin is evenly stretched over the breasts.

In a small bowl, combine the paprika, garlic, salt, pepper, cayenne, and sugar. Sprinkle the spice mix generously over the tops of the stuffed chicken.

Bake until the chicken is cooked through, about 20 to 25 minutes. Transfer the chicken to a cutting board and let stand for 5 minutes, then serve.

• •

Every year, Puritan Poultry provides the Gilmore family with over one hundred turkeys to be served at the Thanksgiving tables of such dignitaries as L.A.'s mayor, police commissioner, and fire chief.

• •

"I love those guys at Puritan Poultry. They carry the best thighs and legs in town; I often use their chicken in my *coq au vin* at the restaurant. They trim the meat to my exact specifications and always get it right."

— Suzanne Tracht, executive chef/owner of Jar and Tracht's

SINGAPORE'S
BANANA LEAF

STALL
122

The stall of Singapore's Banana Leaf might be small, but the flavor of the food is big, and not to be missed. The cuisine of Singapore is a delicious blend of Chinese, Indian, Thai, and Malay cuisines. Family trio Diana and Isaac Gazal and their son, Michael, opened this popular eatery in 2001 after realizing the Market atmosphere was pleasantly similar to an actual Singapore hawker (outdoor food stall). The hybrid wonders of the cuisine were obscure to the owners of Farmers Market, and in true Hollywood style, the Gazals had to audition their specialties for them. They were blown away by the taste of Diana's various delicacies and impressed by her signature approach of showcasing every dish on a banana leaf. And so this cozy gem of a hideaway, with its ceiling fans overhead and its wicker chairs and printed tablecloths, began.

Soon Asians, Malaysians, Indian, and Muslim clientele were flocking to the Market for the real deal of Singaporean-style curries and noodles. Diana came to the United States when she was seventeen years old, with twenty-five dollars, a suitcase, and the ability to cook. She's been in the kitchen all of her life and her commitment to the restaurant and its quality is exceptional. In her mind, the true seal of honorary approval came when the president of Singapore visited and loved the authenticity of her dishes. And it is well-deserved kudos for this mini-powerhouse of a woman who stands all of 4 feet 10 inches tall but is a ball of fire who lets nothing get in the way of her dream or her cooking. The menu's recipes were all developed by her, and the vibrant tastes can be attributed to the curry leaves grown fresh in their home garden, a must-have ingredient in many of the dishes. With Diana on the food front, Isaac in charge of the books, and charming Michael handling public relations, Singapore's Banana Leaf continues to be a happy family affair and best of all, as a team, they put the delicious cuisine of Singapore on the map at the Market.

Mee Goreng (Fried Noodles)

Mee goreng, one of the better known dishes of Singapore, is a standard hawker-stall favorite. *Goreng* means "fried" and *mee* means "noodle"—in this case thin yellow egg noodles. Vermicelli makes a fine substitute if you can't find the real deal. At Singapore's Banana Leaf, the spicy noodles are topped with your choice of tofu, chicken, or the most requested—Indo style—a fried egg.

SERVES 4

2 small russet potatoes

Kosher salt

¾ pound thin yellow egg noodles

6 tablespoons vegetable oil

1 large onion, chopped

4 garlic cloves, minced

1 tablespoon peeled and minced
    fresh ginger

2 large eggs, beaten

½ teaspoon ground turmeric

½ teaspoon sweet paprika

Freshly ground white pepper

¼ cup dark soy sauce

1 cup fresh bean sprouts

4 green onions, white and green parts,
    sliced, plus more for garnish

4 fried eggs (optional)

Crispy fried shallots for garnish (see Note)

1 lime, cut into wedges, for serving

Put the potatoes in a large pot and cover with cold water. Add ½ teaspoon of salt and bring to a boil, uncovered. Simmer until there is no resistance when a fork is inserted into the potatoes, about 20 minutes. Drain the potatoes in a colander. While they are still hot, carefully peel off the skins with a paring knife; use a kitchen towel to hold them. Cut into ½-inch pieces.

In a large pot of boiling salted water, cook the noodles until just tender but still firm to the bite (al dente), about 7 minutes. Take care not to overcook. Rinse under running cool water and drain well. Set aside.

Place a wok or large skillet over medium heat and coat with the oil. When the oil gets hazy, add the onion, garlic, and ginger. Cook and stir until the vegetables are tender but not browned, about 5 minutes. Add the potatoes and continue to cook and stir for 2 minutes to combine and heat through.

Push the vegetables to the sides of the pan and pour the eggs into the center. Scramble the eggs lightly until set, breaking them up into pieces with a spatula. Incorporate the vegetables into the eggs; season with the turmeric, paprika, and salt and pepper to taste.

Add the drained noodles to the wok, stirring and tossing quickly to separate the strands. Pour in the soy sauce, tossing well to coat the noodles and keep them from sticking (drizzle with 1 to 2 tablespoons of water, if necessary). Add the bean sprouts and green onions; cook and stir until softened slightly, about 5 minutes.

Divide the noodles among 4 plates, top with a fried egg, if using, and garnish with sliced green onion and fried shallots. Serve with the lime wedges.

Ingredient Note—Fried Shallots

Crispy fried shallots add a finishing touch to many Asian dishes, particularly those with Thai influence, and often garnish rice and noodle dishes, as well as salads. They are simple to make: Thinly slice 4 or 5 shallots crosswise and separate into rings. Heat 1 inch of vegetable oil in a wok or deep skillet over medium heat. When the oil is hot, fry the shallots until golden, about 3 minutes. Transfer to a plate lined with paper towels to drain. If you don't want to make fried shallots yourself, most Asian markets carry crisp fried shallots in plastic tubs or packets.

Tuna Sambal

In Indonesian and Malaysian cuisine, *sambal* is a piquant dish pleasantly spiked with peppers and chiles. This simple recipe is unique to Singapore's Banana Leaf; Diana created it in her home kitchen as a quick solution for a weeknight supper for her family, using what she had on hand. The result is one of the tastiest items on the menu.

SERVES 4

¼ cup vegetable oil

1 large onion, chopped

4 garlic cloves, minced

1 tablespoon peeled and minced fresh
    ginger

5 tablespoons tomato paste

1 red bell pepper, seeded and thinly sliced

½ teaspoon ground turmeric

½ teaspoon ground cumin

1 tablespoon chile paste such as sambal
    oelek, or 1 fresh green chile, sliced

Sea salt and freshly ground white pepper

3 cans (6 ounces each) solid white tuna,
    packed in water or oil, drained

½ cup coarsely chopped fresh cilantro

Cooked white rice for serving

Place a large skillet over medium heat and coat with the oil. When the oil gets hazy, add the onion, garlic, and ginger. Cook and stir until the vegetables are tender but not browned, about 5 minutes.

Add the tomato paste, bell pepper, turmeric, cumin, and chile paste; season to taste with salt and pepper. Cook and stir until the tomato paste is well incorporated and the peppers are soft, about 5 minutes. Add the tuna, stirring to break it up into flakes and combine. Add about ½ cup of water if the *sambal* looks too dry. Cook for 3 minutes to heat through.

Divide the *sambal* among 4 plates, sprinkle with the cilantro, and serve with the rice.

TUSQUELLAS SEAFOODS

STALL
138

The late John Tusquellas was not only unique among butchers, he was unique among men. He was known as a generous boss who took care of his people and was always fair. John owned the first full-service butcher shop at Farmers Market; in his time, John was considered the patriarch of the group. Standing where Huntington Meats & Sausage (see page 134) is today, Tusquellas Meats was a Market mainstay from 1953 to 1988. John was a first-generation American of Spanish decent who dreamed big and did well. He continued working at his established shop until he was eighty years old, wearing a tie every day.

John passed on his love of the Market to his son Bob, who began working behind the counter as an adolescent slicing bacon. Bob adored the close-knit environment of the Market and hoped to create something of his own here one day. In 1965, after getting a business degree at the University of California, Berkeley, opportunity came knocking. The previous fish market here, Ocean Foods, was reaching the end of its lease and Bob jumped at the chance to plant his own roots at Farmers Market—and work only a stone's throw away from his father. Bob describes that as one of the best times in his life; seeing his father every day was a joy. For over forty years, Tusquellas Seafoods has been carrying not only the finest freshly caught gems from the sea but also daily prepared meals like shrimp cocktail, Asian marinated salmon, and crab-stuffed potatoes. And to keep that spirit of the sea alive, his wife, Kathy, buys him ties with prints of fish on them to complete his "look." When he's there, you'll see Bob working, committed to the task at hand and wearing a tie, just like his dad.

Red Snapper Vera Cruz

This famous dish from coastal Mexico has a light, delicate flavor and is a favorite of Bob's wife, Kathy. Though snapper is classic, any white firm-fleshed fish may be substituted.

SERVES 4

4 red snapper fillets (about 6 ounces each)

Sea salt and freshly ground black pepper

Olive oil for brushing, plus ¼ cup

2 medium onions, thinly sliced

2 garlic cloves, minced

1 can (15 ounces) chopped tomatoes, with juice

2 serrano or jalapeño chiles, finely chopped

1 teaspoon dried oregano

¼ cup coarsely chopped pimiento-stuffed green olives

2 tablespoons capers, drained

Juice of ½ lemon

Chopped fresh flat-leaf parsley for garnish

Cooked white rice for serving

Preheat the oven to 400°F. Season both sides of the snapper fillets with salt and pepper. Brush a 13-by-9-inch baking dish with oil and arrange the fillets side by side in the pan.

Place a skillet over medium heat and coat with the ¼ cup oil. When the oil gets hazy, add the onions. Cook and stir until translucent, about 3 minutes. Add the garlic and cook for 1 minute, stirring. Raise the heat to medium-high and add the tomatoes with their juice, chiles, oregano, olives, capers, and lemon juice. Simmer, uncovered, stirring often, until the sauce thickens slightly, about 5 minutes.

Pour the sauce over the fish. Bake until the fish is opaque throughout, about 15 minutes. Garnish with a shower of chopped parsley and serve with white rice.

193

ULYSSES VOYAGE

STALL
750

Greece and its sun-kissed isles features a tantalizing cuisine that is fresh and fragrant, served with warmth and vitality. The Greeks' zest for the good life and love of simple, well-seasoned foods is reflected at the table. This is certainly the case at Ulysses Voyage, the Greek *taverna* situated just outside the Market's plaza and owned by Peter and Hanna Carabatsos. Born and raised in Athens, Peter has always been surrounded by food. His grandparents ran a traditional Greek coffee house in Athens. At the *cafenio*, they served not only coffee but also simple *mezethes*, or small plates, to provide the backdrop for social gatherings. Peter's mother, Mama Voula, inherited a passion for cooking. He says, "My mother was born into the pot. She is a real creator with food, and cooks to relax."

When Peter brought his wife-to-be, Hanna, to Athens to meet Mama, they came up with the concept to open a restaurant in Los Angeles. Peter jokes, "When you drink a lot of ouzo, good ideas come into your head!" To him, the Market has always felt like those in Europe where people could walk, talk, and grab a bite with friends. When the time came, he couldn't imagine a more fitting location for his family's Mediterranean oasis. In 2003, he opened Ulysses Voyage. In doing so, he has brought Greece to the Market, with old-world values in a new-world setting. Peter is proud of the over eighty homemade items on his menu. In fact, Mama Voula came to Los Angeles to teach chef Frank Torres all of her recipes. Their clientele runs the gamut, but Peter is most proud of the gold-star response from the Greek community, who say the food reminds them of their mothers' cooking. He also has created an impressive list of Greek wines and ouzos. With a cry of "*Opa!*" Peter celebrates his success and is delighted to bring the tastes of his Hellenic homeland to Hollywood.

Mama Voula's Spanakopita

Spanakopita is a Greek spinach pie that has become one of the most beloved dishes on the menu. In addition to being a satisfying vegetarian entree, you can cut the casserole into small squares and serve as a substantial appetizer.

3 tablespoons extra-virgin olive oil, preferably Greek, plus more for brushing

6 leeks, white and light green parts, chopped and well rinsed

4 garlic cloves, minced

2½ pounds fresh baby spinach, rinsed and dried

½ teaspoon freshly ground black pepper

2 cups crumbled firm feta cheese, preferably Greek

½ cup finely chopped fresh dill

½ cup finely chopped fresh mint

3 large eggs, lightly beaten

2 frozen country-style filo sheets or puff pastry sheets (see Note), thawed but kept chilled

Preheat the oven to 350°F.

Place a large skillet over medium-high heat and coat with the 3 tablespoons of oil. When the oil is hazy, add the leeks and garlic; cook and stir until fragrant and very soft, about 4 minutes. Add the spinach in handfuls, folding the leaves under with a spoon as you add each batch. Let the spinach wilt and cook down before adding more. Once all the spinach is in the pan, season with the pepper.

Remove from the heat and transfer the spinach mixture to a colander over the sink. Using the back of a spoon, gently press out all of the excess liquid. Set aside to cool; the filling needs to cool down a bit to prevent the dough from becoming soggy. Once the spinach mixture is cool, put it in a bowl and add the feta, dill, mint, and eggs. Fold the ingredients together until well combined.

Brush the bottom and sides of a 9-by-13-inch baking dish with oil. Working with 1 sheet at a time, lay the dough on a lightly floured surface and roll it out slightly to fit the pan. Line the bottom of the dish with the first piece of dough, pressing into the

corners. Trim off any excess with a paring knife. Spread the spinach filling evenly over the dough. Cover with the second sheet of dough, trimming around the edges of the dish. Brush the top with oil.

Bake until the top is puffed and golden brown, about 30 to 35 minutes. Let stand for 10 minutes before cutting into squares. Serve warm or at room temperature.

Ingredient Note—Filo

In the villages of Greece, filo dough is typically rolled out by hand, but unless you are very accomplished, it's nearly impossible to stretch it as thin as it is produced by machine. Mama Voula makes her spinach pie as it is served in her native village of Kalamata, with a slightly thicker filo instead of the typical tissue-thin sheets. Sold under the label "country-style filo" (called *horiatiko* in Greek), the sheets are thicker and more elastic than the usual thin and fragile filo. If country-style filo is not available in your market's freezer section, go ahead and substitute puff pastry.

197

Salmon Plaki with Lemon Potatoes

The beauty of the Greek islands is that all of the glorious seafood is locally caught and eaten shortly after. The fresh catch of the day is typically either grilled or made into a *plaki* in Greece. *Plaki*, meaning "to bake with tomatoes," is a preparation used in every home and restaurant. Experiment with different types of fish, like flounder, halibut, or even a whole striped bass. At Ulysses Voyage, Mama Voula features salmon because of its popularity. Serve your favorite green vegetable alongside the Lemon Potatoes.

SERVES 4

4 salmon fillets (about 8 ounces each)

Sea salt and freshly ground black pepper

Olive oil, preferably Greek, for brushing,
     plus ¼ cup

1 large onion, sliced

Needles of 2 rosemary sprigs, chopped

½ cup dry white wine such as Sauvignon
     Blanc

2 cups peeled, chopped, fresh plum (Roma)
     tomatoes, plus 2 plum (Roma) tomatoes,
     seeded and diced, for garnish

Chopped fresh flat-leaf parsley for garnish

Lemon Potatoes (recipe follows) for
     serving

Preheat the oven to 350°F. Season both sides of the salmon fillets with salt and pepper. Brush a 13-by-9-inch baking dish with oil and arrange the fillets side by side in the pan.

Place a skillet over medium heat and coat with the ¼ cup oil. When the oil gets hazy, add the onion and rosemary. Cook and stir until the onion is translucent and fragrant, about 3 minutes. Season to taste with salt and pepper. Pour in the wine and cook until the liquid is almost totally evaporated, about 1 minute. Stir in the 2 cups tomatoes. Simmer, uncovered, stirring often, until the sauce thickens slightly, about 5 minutes.

Pour the sauce over the salmon. Bake until the fish is slightly firm but still pink inside, about 15 minutes. Garnish with a sprinkling of diced tomatoes and parsley. Serve with the Lemon Potatoes.

LEMON POTATOES

Known in Greece as *ellinikos*, these lemon potatoes may be basic but they are nonetheless delicate and delicious. With hints of lemon, garlic, and herbs, they're hard to resist.

SERVES 4

2 pounds Yukon gold potatoes, scrubbed
   and quartered

6 garlic cloves, minced

2 teaspoons dried Greek oregano

Sea salt and freshly ground black pepper

1 cup freshly squeezed lemon juice, or as
   needed

½ cup olive oil

About 2 cups water or low-sodium
   chicken broth

Chopped fresh flat-leaf parsley for garnish

Preheat the oven to 350°F.

Put the potatoes in a baking dish and scatter the garlic and oregano over the top. Season to taste with salt and pepper. Pour in the 1 cup lemon juice, oil, and 2 cups water. Add more lemon juice or water as needed to submerge the potatoes at least halfway up the sides. Cover with aluminum foil and bake for 40 minutes. Remove the foil and continue to bake until the potatoes are fork-tender, about 20 minutes longer. With a slotted spoon, arrange the potatoes on a platter. Garnish with a shower of chopped parsley and serve.

199

sweet things

chapter **4**

Peanut Brittle, page 230

Farmers Market is at its most vibrant after dark, especially during the holiday season when the clock tower is festively decorated and all lit up. After catching a movie next door at the Grove, couples and families alike mosey over to Farmers Market for a scoop of homemade ice cream, to sample a slice of pie, or perhaps buy a lucky lottery ticket at one of the newsstands. The Market officially closes at 9:00 P.M. but many of the merchants stay open a bit later to accommodate the young night dwellers. Both beer and wine bars at Farmers Market, 326 and E.B.'s, serve until 11:00 P.M. and get pretty lively in the evening. Groups of friends often hang out while sampling a little pastry. The nighttime atmosphere is fun, friendly, and laid-back. This old-fashioned marketplace invites the new generation to become part of a community that embraces a come-as-you-are attitude and to escape the frantic urban lifestyle of present-day Los Angeles. There is no other destination in the city like Farmers Market, where the intersection of a modern, young culture merges with the traditions of past generations to create a truly original communal space.

BENNETT'S ICE CREAM

STALL
548

In the family tree of life and business, the luscious legacy of an ice-cream dynasty could be as sweet as it gets. Scott Bennett is the third generation of Bennett men to work at the Market and the second to keep his family's popular ice-cream stand alive and flourishing. Scott's grandfather, Murray H. Bennett, was Farmers Market manager from 1947 to 1968. As a result, Murray was privy to the fact that the Silveras family was selling their ice-cream shop, and he encouraged his son Chuck to buy it. In 1963, with the help of his father, Chuck created Bennett's Ice Cream. Murray pushed their dream forward by taking out a second mortgage on his house. Chuck worked hard making quality ice cream, and, within two years, he paid back not only the second mortgage but the first as well.

Scott Bennett's future in ice cream was destined when he started working for his favorite uncle at the parlor at just six years old. He considers Chuck to be the most influential force in his life, saying his uncle made him the successful businessman he is today. He smiles fondly when he recounts some of his uncle's philosophical gems such as, "A fast nickel beats a slow dime," "Make good food at a fair price, and you'll make a living," and "Do it right; do it once." When Chuck

passed in 1992, Scott inherited Bennett's and the Refresher (see page 233). Today, he oversees the creamy Bennett enterprise, where twenty-four fresh flavors of ice cream are churned on the premises five days a week. Signature favorites are Choffee Choffee (chocolate-and-coffee and chocolate-and-toffee combined), pumpkin, and Fancy Nancy, an ode to his wife.

203

Fancy Nancy Ice Cream

Ever since Scott Bennett started dating his wife, Nancy, she loved to eat coffee ice cream topped with sliced bananas and a drizzle of caramel sauce. Being the romantic, Scott invented a love-letter flavor to match his wife's affections. Their son, Charlie, came up with the catchy moniker, and Fancy Nancy has been a favorite ever since. There is something extra-special about homemade ice cream, and this recipe could not be simpler.

MAKES 1 QUART

2 cups cold heavy cream

1 cup cold whole milk

¾ cup sugar, plus 1 tablespoon

3 tablespoons freeze-dried instant coffee
   crystals

1 teaspoon pure vanilla extract

¼ teaspoon unflavored gelatin

Pinch of salt

2 ripe bananas

2 cups caramel sauce, chilled

Pour the cream, milk, and ¾ cup sugar into the freezer bowl of an ice-cream machine. Add the coffee, vanilla, gelatin, and salt. Churn according to the manufacturer's directions. Chop up the bananas with the 1 tablespoon sugar to make a paste about the consistency of baby food. About 5 minutes before freezing/mixing ends, add the bananas. Continue to churn until combined but still chunky, about 2 minutes longer. When done, the ice cream will have a soft-serve consistency.

Getting caramel ribbons throughout the batch takes a little finesse. First, transfer the ice cream to a tall container and pour the caramel sauce on top. Using a ladle or long rubber spatula, fold the caramel down to the bottom and slowly bring it back up in another spot to create swirls. Do this several times, until there are caramel ribbons running throughout the whole batch.

To harden the ice cream fully, cover, and freeze until firm, at least 3 hours. Use within 1 month.

ICE
COLD
DRINKS

Bennetts

HOME MADE ICE CREAM

ICE CREAM MADE HERE

COME TASTE SOME GREAT ICE CREAM

Cabernet Sauvignon Sorbet

Don't drive after you've had this sweet treat. It takes two of people's favorite indulgences, wine and dessert, and whips them together into a refreshing, barely sweet palate cleanser. In 2002, Bennett's took home top honors at the L.A. County Fair for this unique garnet-colored sorbet. The beauty of this sorbet is that you can serve it straight from the freezer as the alcohol gives it a nice soft consistency. Blackberries make a great pairing, if you want to top with some fresh fruit.

MAKES 1 QUART

Simple Syrup

1 cup sugar

2 cups water

1 cup Cabernet Sauvignon, chilled

¼ teaspoon unflavored gelatin

1 tablespoon fresh lemon juice or
citric acid

To make the simple syrup: Combine the sugar and water in a pot over medium heat. Bring to a gentle simmer and cook, stirring, until the sugar is totally dissolved and the liquid goes from cloudy to clear, about 2 minutes. Do not allow the syrup to boil or get dark. Remove from the heat and let the syrup cool completely, then refrigerate until very cold, about 2 hours, before using. You should have about 2½ cups. Simple syrup can be stored in the refrigerator indefinitely kept in a covered container.

In a large bowl, combine the cold simple syrup, wine, gelatin, and lemon juice. Pour the wine mixture into an ice-cream machine and churn according to the manufacturer's directions. When done, the sorbet will have a slushy consistency. To harden the sorbet fully, transfer to a container, cover, and freeze until firm, at least 3 hours. Use within 1 month.

207

BREADWORKS

STALL
330

Breadworks at Farmers Market is a testament to two men's lifelong devotion to baking artisanal bread. Meir Jacobs (better known as Mickey) first worked in a bakery as a fifteen-year-old boy in Budapest in 1935. From then on, he never strayed from the bakery business. He moved to Los Angeles in 1970 and purchased nearby Browns Bakery, then opened the J&T (Jacobs & Tajkef) Bread Bin at Farmers Market in 1973. In the same location at Farmers Market for over thirty-five years, Mickey has continually served an incredible selection of breads and pastries to his devoted customers. Even at eighty-six years old, Mickey is still an integral part of this seven-day-a-week operation, now owned by Seth Silverman's Breadworks Bakery.

A born-and-bred Angeleno, Seth got his start in the business at La Brea Bakery, the number-one artisan bread purveyor in North America. He always dreamed about owning his own shop, and eventually his dream came true. Originally located on Third Street (just a block from Farmers Market), Breadworks had been serving baked goods to the greater L.A. community for fifteen years. Seth took ownership in 2005 and has continued to work and grow with the same bakers that have been part of the Breadworks family for years. Under Seth's direction, the shop has grown into a full-service bakery, creating delicious, distinctive breads, pastries, and traditional Jewish delicacies for grateful eaters throughout the city and beyond. The operation recently merged with Brown's Bakery, which is where Seth's relationship with Mickey developed. Using nothing but the finest ingredients, Mickey and Seth have created several unique signature breads, such as the Cinnamon Loaf and hand-formed cookies like their Almond Horns.

Hungarian Cinnamon Loaf

This bread is Mickey's pride and joy. It is made by hand and has a crust on top like no other. Breadworks sells about twenty loaves every day. Try it for French toast.

MAKES ONE 9-BY-5-INCH LOAF

1 package (¼ ounce) active dry yeast

1¼ cups warm milk

1 cup sugar

1 cup (2 sticks) unsalted butter, melted
 and cooled, plus more for brushing

3 large egg yolks

1 teaspoon salt

3½ cups all-purpose flour, plus more for
 dusting

2 tablespoons ground cinnamon

In the bowl of a standing electric mixer fitted with the dough hook, dissolve the yeast in ¼ cup of the warm milk. Sprinkle with a pinch of the sugar and let the mixture stand until the yeast comes alive and starts to foam, about 5 to 10 minutes.

Turn the mixer on low speed and add the remaining 1 cup milk, ½ cup of the sugar, the 1 cup melted butter, the egg yolks, and salt. Add 2 cups of the flour and turn the speed up to medium; continue to mix until incorporated. Gradually add the remaining 1½ cups flour and continue to mix until the dough holds together and pulls away from the sides of the bowl; the dough will be very soft.

Turn the dough out onto a lightly floured work surface and knead until smooth and elastic, about 10 minutes. Put the dough in a large bowl. Cover with a kitchen towel or plastic wrap and let rise in a warm place until doubled in size, about 1½ hours. Test the dough by pressing 2 fingers into it. If indents remain, the dough is adequately risen.

Combine the remaining ½ cup sugar and the cinnamon in a small bowl. Brush the bottom and sides of a 9-by-5-inch loaf pan with melted butter.

On a lightly floured work surface, roll the dough into a rectangle about the size of the loaf pan. Brush the surface of the dough with melted butter and sprinkle the cinnamon sugar evenly across. Roll the dough up, jelly-roll style, into a long cylinder, and pinch the seam closed. Put the dough in the prepared loaf pan, seam-side down. Make sure the dough touches all sides of the pan. Cover with plastic wrap and let rise a second time, until the top of the dough is nearly level with the top of the loaf pan, about 20 minutes.

Preheat the oven to 350°F. Brush the dough with melted butter.

Bake until your kitchen smells like cinnamon and the bread is golden brown, 45 minutes to 1 hour. Let cool in the pan for 5 minutes, then turn out onto a wire rack to cool completely.

"I can't resist the poppyseed hamentashen at Breadworks bakery. The tender cookies have an authentic, old-world flavor about them and are even better the next day when the poppyseeds seep into the cookie and soften it a bit."
— Sherry Yard, executive pastry chef of Spago Beverly Hills

Almond Horns

In addition to their sensational breads, Breadworks offers an array of cookies and baked treats. Their authentic old-world almond horn is a local favorite. Pure almond paste is the key ingredient. It contains less sugar than marzipan, which gives the cookies a stronger nut flavor.

MAKES 1 DOZEN COOKIES

1 can (8 ounces) almond paste

1 cup sugar

2 large eggs

1 teaspoon almond extract

½ cup all-purpose flour, plus more for dusting

1 cup sliced almonds

2 cups finely chopped semisweet chocolate or morsels

Preheat the oven to 350°F. Line 2 baking pans with parchment paper.

Put the almond paste and sugar in a food processor and pulse until the mixture is the texture of fine crumbs. Add the eggs and almond extract and process until the mixture is very smooth. Add the flour and process until the dough is very sticky.

Turn the dough out onto a heavily floured work surface. Roll the dough into a 1-foot-long log. Divide the dough into 12 equal pieces and roll into balls. Roll the balls into 3-inch logs, slightly tapered at the ends. Curve the logs into a crescent shape. Spread the almonds on a plate. Press both sides of the cookie into the almonds.

Put the almond horns side by side on the prepared pans. Bake until the edges are lightly golden, about 20 minutes. Transfer to wire racks and let cool completely.

While the cookies are cooling, put the chopped chocolate in a microwave-safe dish and microwave on high power for 1 minute, stirring every 20 seconds. If additional time is needed, check at 10-second intervals. Stir the chocolate constantly until it is shiny and completely smooth.

Dip the ends of the cookies into the melted chocolate and place on a baking pan. Let stand until the chocolate is set.

COUNTRY BAKERY

STALL
530

Having a piece of pie from the Country Bakery is like being at a country fair bake-off and enjoying the blue-ribbon winner. Owner and baker Bill Thee has been making pies at this bakery stand since 1988 and no matter what the flavors, all are delectable with their flaky homemade crusts and mouthwatering fillings. Being the pastry specialist that he is, Bill always aspires to making and baking the best of the best, with the finest natural ingredients available. And on top of that, he's found a way to satisfy everyone's sweet tooth, no matter what the preference, reason, or occasion. His European-style bakery, Thee's Continental Pastries (see page 240), offers an impressive assortment of refined and elegant old-world delights, while the Country Bakery features all of his Americana favorites. His perfect pies are only a part of his ever-expanding rustic repertoire. Take note of the bakery's famous alligator cinnamon pecan danish, its fabulous funnel cakes, or the perfectly plump apple dumplings. All of the baked goods are beautifully prepared, and each bite is well worth savoring and lingering over just like a memorable delicious day at a county fair.

SWEET THINGS

Apple Dumplings

The marriage of apples and pastry is a familiar, comforting one. Dumplings are a bit homier than the typical apple pie or tart and very easy to make. Choose crisp baking apples, such as Granny Smith or pippin, and be sure to peel them just prior to baking to avoid browning. This is one of the Country Bakery's biggest sellers.

SERVES 4

1 recipe Pie Pastry (page 216)

2 large eggs, beaten

4 Granny Smith or pippin apples, peeled and cored but left whole

4 maraschino cherries

½ cup granulated sugar

1 tablespoon ground cinnamon

1 cup confectioners' sugar

¼ cup hot water

Heavy cream or ice cream for serving

Preheat the oven to 400°F. Line a baking pan with parchment paper.

On a lightly floured work surface, roll the pastry out into a rectangle and cut evenly into four 6-inch squares. Gather up the scraps and roll out again. Using a 3-inch ring cutter, cut out 4 circles. Brush the surface of the pastry with some of the beaten eggs.

Place an apple in the center of each square of dough. Stuff the core of each apple with a cherry. In a small bowl, combine the granulated sugar and cinnamon. Fill the apple centers with the cinnamon sugar. Bring the corners of the dough up to cover the apples and pinch the edges to seal. Set the pastry rounds on top of the apple dumplings like a little hat. Brush the dumplings with the beaten eggs. Put the apple dumplings in the prepared pan. Bake the dumplings until the pastry is golden brown and the apples are tender but not dissolved into apple sauce, 30 to 35 minutes.

Put the confectioners' sugar in a bowl and slowly pour in the hot water, stirring until the sugar is a pourable consistency. Drizzle over the apple dumplings and let cool slightly so the icing is hardened before serving. Serve warm with the heavy cream.

215

Banana Cream Pie

This is one pie you don't want to toss in somebody's face. Baker Bill Thee is famous for his freshly baked pies. One of his favorite desserts as a child, and still today, is banana cream pie. There is no hint of packaged pudding in this recipe, only the flavor of silky homemade vanilla custard sweet with the taste of ripe bananas.

SERVES 8

Pie Pastry

2 cups all-purpose flour, plus more for
    dusting

2 tablespoons sugar

1 teaspoon salt

¾ cup (1½ sticks) cold unsalted butter,
    cut into small chunks

2 tablespoons ice water, plus more if
    needed

Filling

¾ cup sugar

3 tablespoons cornstarch

3 large eggs

1 tablespoon pure vanilla extract

2½ cups milk

2 tablespoons unsalted butter, cut into
    small pieces

Whipped Cream

1 cup cold heavy cream

1 teaspoon pure vanilla extract

¼ cup confectioners' sugar

2 bananas, sliced

To make the pie pastry: Combine the 2 cups flour, the sugar, and salt in a large bowl. Add the butter and mix with a pastry blender or your hands until the mixture resembles coarse crumbs. Pour in the 2 tablespoons ice water; work it in to bind the dough until it holds together without being too wet or sticky. Squeeze a small amount together; if it is crumbly, add more ice water, 1 teaspoon at a time. Form the dough into a disc and wrap in plastic wrap; refrigerate for at least 30 minutes. (Feel free to make the dough the night before if you prefer.)

Preheat the oven to 400°F.

On a lightly floured work surface, roll the dough into a large circle about ⅛ inch thick. Place a 9-inch pie plate upside down on top and trim with a knife, leaving 2 inches extra dough all the way around. Lay the dough circle in the pan and gently press the crust into place. Fold the excess dough inside the rim and crimp the edges.

Prick the bottom of the dough with a fork. Lay a piece of aluminum foil on the bottom of the dough and fill it with 2 cups of dried beans. The weight of the beans will keep the pastry dough flat so it doesn't bubble while you prebake it. Put the pan on a baking pan so it will be easier to move in and out of the oven.

Bake the crust until it begins to brown, about 15 minutes. Lift out the beans in the foil and return the crust to the oven. Bake until golden brown, about 15 minutes longer. Remove the crust from the oven and let cool.

To make the filling: In a bowl, combine half of the sugar with the cornstarch. Add the eggs, 1 at a time, whisking thoroughly after each addition until the mixture is lump free. Stir in the vanilla.

Combine the milk and remaining sugar in a 3-quart pot and place over medium heat. Stir constantly until the milk mixture begins to thicken and reaches just below the simmering point, about 8 minutes. While constantly whisking, slowly drizzle the hot milk into the egg mixture (do not add too quickly or the eggs will scramble). Return the tempered eggs back into the pot and whisk constantly until the custard comes to a boil and is thick enough to coat the back of a spoon, about 5 minutes. It should be much like the consistency of pudding. Remove from the heat and whisk in the butter until completely melted. Let cool slightly.

To make the whipped cream: Whisk together the heavy cream and vanilla in a bowl. Sprinkle in the sugar and whip until the cream mounds on itself.

Pour the custard filling into the cooled pie shell. Push the banana slices below the surface to prevent them from browning, and then smooth the top with a spatula. Cover with plastic wrap and refrigerate at least 4 hours or overnight. Top with the whipped cream before serving.

FARM BOY

Pretty as a painting, the pure beauty and impressive displays of the fresh fruits and vegetables at Farm Boy cannot escape notice. Owner Peter Chae takes great pride in the prime quality and the eye-appeal of his pristine produce; it almost looks too good to eat. For everything from the perfect plum to ravishing rhubarb, bountiful berries, or stellar stone fruit, Farm Boy is like a California dream, perfectly seasonal, fresh, and inspiring. As one of the newest vendors to join the Farmers Market family, Peter took over the stall from longtime grocer Dave Shimotani of the Fruit Company in 2008. Peter's life has always been about the grocery business. He came to the United States from Seoul, South Korea, at the age of twenty-six and went to work for his buddy who owned a

boutique market to learn the ropes. While there, he cultivated his own knowledge, especially when it came to produce. Soon after, he realized he valued the personable approach of the smaller marketplace and as a result, he opened his first Farm Boy in 1993. Peter is known for the standards he demands for his clientele. For him, a successful business is that simple: top quality fruits and vegetables, hands-on service, and a stellar presentation. With Peter Chae as the utmost professional and the artist behind the scenes, Farm Boy is a picture-perfect-produce masterpiece.

=SWEET=

MANGOS

$1.98 EA

Summer Berry Crumble

Farm Boy carries a rainbow of berries, and this recipe shows off their natural sweetness in style. Filled with flavor, loaded with nutrition, and bursting with juice, they are a dessert maker's dream. If you prefer, you can make the cobbler in a soufflé dish or casserole; bake for 40 minutes.

SERVES 4

2 pints fresh berries such as strawberries, raspberries, blueberries, or blackberries or a combination

¼ cup granulated sugar

Pinch of salt

1 tablespoon cornstarch

Juice and finely grated zest of 1 lemon

Streusel Topping

1 cup all-purpose flour, sifted

½ cup quick-cooking oats

½ cup loosely packed light brown sugar

¼ teaspoon salt

1 teaspoon pure vanilla extract

¼ cup (½ stick) cold unsalted butter, cut into small chunks

Vanilla ice cream for serving

Preheat the oven to 400°F.

In a bowl, combine the berries with the granulated sugar, salt, cornstarch, and lemon juice and zest. Fold gently to combine. Let stand for 5 minutes while you make the streusel topping.

To make the streusel topping: Combine the flour, oats, brown sugar, salt, and vanilla in a bowl. Add the butter and, using your fingers, work it in until the mixture resembles coarse crumbs. Do not overmix.

Divide the berry mixture among 4 eight-ounce ramekins. Put the topping on the berries to cover and arrange the cobblers on a baking pan. Bake until the topping is golden brown and the fruit juices are bubbling, 20 to 25 minutes. Serve warm with the vanilla ice cream.

221

GILL'S OLD-FASHIONED ICE CREAM

I scream. You scream. We all should scream for Gill's Old-Fashioned Ice Cream, one of the oldest and most established stands at the Market, founded by Joe Gill in the spring of 1938. Son Bob began behind the counter as a kid scooping ice cream on weekends, and in some form or fashion, he's been at it ever since. Today, Gill's is still serving ice cream, and Bob's personal touches are more than apparent. He is proud to let you know that he was the first stand in L.A. to serve homemade spumoni, and he's gone on to become the connoisseur of elaborate, enticing-to-look-at (and even better to eat) ice-cream sculptures and cakes. Using individual pewter molds, Gill's ice cream is pushed and shaped into various edible custom-made

designs. The molds are hinged and heavy so that they hold the cold temperature longer. His vintage collection of ice-cream molds features an array of fruit shapes, from apples and bananas to strawberries, plums, and peaches. More often than not, the flavor of ice cream is the same as the fruit it represents, and Bob's frozen fruit basket is as eye-catching as it is delicious.

Many other fun forms of molded ice cream have been proudly made for customers for all occasions throughout the year. Around the holidays, look out for ice-cream-shaped turkeys made with chocolate or pumpkin ice cream. Over the years, Bob has been clever in merging an old-fashioned ice-cream parlor with the modern day, so whether on a cone or in a slice, Gill's Old-Fashioned Ice Cream will leave your taste buds screaming for more.

Gill's old fas

FLAVORS
VANILLA
CHOC
STRAW
COFFEE
CHOC CHIP
BANANA NUT
ROCKY ROAD
MINT CHIP
PEPPERMIN
PISTACHIO
PINE. COC
UTTER PECA
COOKIES 'N
NEAPOLITAN
CHOC. MALT

SORBETS
LEMON
RASPBERRY
ORANGE
SHERBET

Coke 3

Coca-Cola
CLASSIC

Fresh
LIMEADE

Spa

If the site of Gill's ice-cream counter seems slightly familiar, don't be surprised. Renowned lifestyle photographer Henri Cartier-Bresson saw the beauty of the Market and snapped one of his most famous intimate portraits here. The award-winning 1947 image of a cozy couple happens to be that of Johnny and Sheila Gill, Bob's brother and sister-in-law!

Limeade

Although a popular beverage in the summertime, Gill's county-style limeade is enjoyed year-round. The lip-smacking lime flavor adds an extra zing that typical lemonade doesn't have. Bob Gill wouldn't even think of using bottled lime juice; thirty-year employee Carlos Villa still hand squeezes cases of bright green limes fresh every day . . . he's got the twist of the wrist to get every last drop.

Note, the recipe begins with a simple syrup, a mixture of sugar and water used frequently as a sweetener in beverages. It's easiest to make the simple syrup in advance; it can be used in the preparation of many refreshing coolers and cocktails and stored indefinitely in the refrigerator. This quantity of simple syrup will be enough to temper the tart acidity of the lime juice without being overly sweet.

SERVES 4

Simple Syrup	1 cup fresh lime juice (about 8 limes)
1 cup sugar	1 quart filtered water, or as needed
1 cup water	Ice cubes
	Lime slices for garnish
	Fresh mint springs for garnish (optional)

To make Simple Syrup: Combine the sugar and water in a small pot over medium heat. Bring to a gentle simmer and cook, stirring, until the sugar is totally dissolved and the liquid goes from cloudy to clear, about 2 minutes. Do not allow the syrup to boil or get dark. Remove from the heat and let the syrup cool completely. You should have about 1½ cups of simple syrup.

In a pitcher, mix the cooled syrup with the lime juice and stir to combine. (You can refrigerate the limeade concentrate at this point for up to 5 days.) Add 1 quart water and stir to mix well. If you desire a little less tartness and sweetness, just add more water to taste.

To serve, fill tall glasses with ice and pour in the limeade. Garnish with slices of lime and mint, if desired.

Ingredient Note—Fresh Lime Juice

For juicing, buy limes that are not completely hard and give slightly to palm pressure. Softer limes generally have thinner rinds and more juice. Before juicing the limes, roll them on the counter while pressing down with your palm to help break down the interior membranes and make juicing easier. Then cut them in half along the equator and press and twist against a reamer or hand juicer to extract the juice. Pass the lime juice through a fine-mesh strainer if you don't like pulp. For ease, you should plan to have the juice end up in a measuring cup when you are done juicing and straining. For easy storage, freeze the lime concentrate in ice cube trays.

Variations—Slushies and Fizzies

Process fresh lime ice cubes in a blender or food processor to make a delicious lime slushie. If you're in the mood for a fizzy drink, substitute a snazzy seltzer or sparkling water for the flat water.

227

LITTLEJOHN'S ENGLISH TOFFEE HOUSE

STALL
432

Littlejohn's Candies was started in the Los Angeles area in the 1920s by Mr. and Mrs. Littlejohn. After twenty years of successfully catering to the elite of L.A., they moved the storefront and kitchen to Farmers Market in 1946. Well known for their mouthwatering English toffee, they named the new location Littlejohn's English Toffee House. While the store has changed ownership over the years, the foundation that the Littlejohns crafted is still in place today; in fact, most of the kitchen equipment is original from the '40s. Mr. and Mrs. Littlejohn passed the candy shop down to Bill Bishop in 1976, who continued to make candy in the time-honored tradition of small batches and premium ingredients.

Bill, coming from a family of candy makers, had learned the craft from his father in his early years before working at Littlejohn's. As a teenager, Mike Graves apprenticed with Bill to begin the next generation of candy makers and has never left. After years of perfecting his artistry through hands-on training, Mike bought Littlejohn's in 1983. With more than twenty-five years of making candy to his credit, Mike has been unwavering in the quality and consistency of each batch. He continues the custom of hand-stirring over open flames in copper kettles, working each confection to perfection on marble tables and using only the freshest natural ingredients. On any given day, you can see Mike at work through the windows of the kitchen creating mouthwatering fudge, English toffee, caramel, and seasonal favorites like chocolate Easter bunnies and heart-shaped Valentine boxes. The candy window provides a prime view of the Market. In fact, Mike first spotted his wife Colleen through the window. She was staring at him as he was dipping chocolate, they exchanged glances, and as Mike puts it, "she had a particular smile about her." History has a way of repeating itself—Mike's parents also met at Farmers Market.

Peanut Brittle

Sweet, but not sticky. Kind of buttery, but never greasy. Hard, but not tough. Thin and translucent. Aromatic, infused with the flavor of roasted peanuts. These are the qualities of unforgettable peanut brittle. Littlejohn's English Toffee House is almost as famous for its brittle as it is for its signature toffee. Master candy maker Mike Graves insists the peanuts should be raw Spanish peanuts, with the skins on. Raw, because they are actually roasted in the syrup as it cooks, infusing the candy with color and flavor.

MAKES ABOUT 1 POUND

½ cup water

1 cup sugar

½ cup light corn syrup

1 teaspoon salt

1 cup raw Spanish peanuts

2 tablespoons unsalted butter, at room temperature

Pinch of baking soda

Preheat the oven to 250°F. Place a baking pan in the oven to preheat as well. The hot pan allows you a little time to spread the brittle evenly and thinly without it hardening.

Combine the water, sugar, corn syrup, and salt in a 3-quart pot over medium heat. Cook and stir until the sugar dissolves, 2 to 3 minutes. Stir slowly with a wooden spoon until the sugar mixture comes to a gentle boil, about 5 minutes. Keep an eye on the pot; the mixture will get bubbly. Wash down the inside wall of the pot with a wet pastry brush if sugar crystals start to form. Continue stirring until the mixture is light amber and reaches between 250 and 260°F on a candy thermometer, or until a small amount of syrup dropped into cold water forms a rigid ball, about 15 minutes.

Add the peanuts and raise the heat slightly. The peanuts will clump up a bit at first but as you cook and stir they even out. Continue stirring until the mixture reaches 295°F; the color should be deep golden brown. Stir in the butter until completely melted but not burned. Remove from the heat. Add the baking soda and stir briskly to blend; the mixture will foam up.

Carefully pour onto the hot baking pan and spread it thinly and evenly with a metal spatula, making sure the peanuts are in a single layer. Stretch until the brittle is thinner than the peanuts, about ¼ inch thick. You will have to work quickly when pouring out and spreading the mixture in the pan.

Let the brittle cool completely at room temperature. When the brittle is hard, break it into pieces. Store in an airtight container at room temperature for up to 2 weeks.

"I always bring out-of-town guests to Farmers Market because everyone can find something different to eat. When I'm there, I stop by Littlejohn's to pick up their divinity candy. It's one of the only places I can get it in town."

— Josie LeBalch, executive chef/owner of Josie

231

Chocolate Fudge

Candy maker Mike Graves makes over twenty pounds of decadent fudge per day! Littlejohn's has about a dozen varieties. Handmade from scratch the old-fashioned way using only the finest ingredients, fudge is perfect to enjoy yourself or give as a gift.

MAKES 2 POUNDS

2 cups sweetened condensed milk

2 cups sugar

½ cup (1 stick) salted butter, plus more
    for greasing

3 tablespoons corn syrup

4 ounces unsweetened chocolate,
    coarsely chopped

1 teaspoon pure vanilla extract

1 cup chopped roasted nuts (optional)

Butter an 8-by-12-inch glass baking dish. A candy maker's trick is to line the pan with a sheet of wax paper to facilitate removal after the fudge cools.

In a heavy-bottomed pot over medium-high heat, combine the milk, sugar, butter, and corn syrup. Bring to a boil as quickly as possible, stirring with a wooden spoon. Boil until the mixture is very thick, about 10 minutes. Remove from the heat.

Mix in the chocolate and vanilla. Stir or whisk until the chocolate is fully melted and well incorporated. The batch will thicken up drastically; stir until just beyond when the thickening is readily apparent. Fold in the nuts, if using.

Pour into the prepared baking dish. Score the fudge with a knife. Wait until the fudge cools and is firm and then cut all the way through into squares. Store the fudge in an airtight container or plastic wrap to prevent it from drying out. For short periods (1 or 2 weeks), room temperature is fine. Store in the refrigerator for up to 1 month; any longer, pop it into the freezer.

THE REFRESHER

After creating successful Bennett's Ice Cream (see page 203), owner Chuck Bennett, being the entrepreneur that he was, realized there was very little around to wash down the amazing food at the Market. In order to supplement the food stands with drink, he opened this soda shop as a secondary store in 1970. He designed the stand like an old-time fountain shop, equipped with an old-fashioned cash register manufactured in 1948. The Refresher, appropriately named after the Coca-Cola company newsletter, had a humble start with a solid following when it sold only Coca-Cola products and frozen bananas. Today, it still goes through two cases of bananas a week.

When Chuck's nephew, Scott Bennett, inherited the business in 1992, he updated the soda shop to include boutique, esoteric, and regional sodas from around the county and international sodas from around the world. He has since created a niche soda shop, a welcome throwback to days gone by, mixing the old with the new and the cool with the retro in bottles and selections. He features such fruit sodas as black cherry, peach, pineapple, banana, and orange. Seeking out unique flavors that could become sparkling gems has become his fun hobby. He's even tried his hand at manufacturing his own sodas. Scott currently offers three of his own creations with labels designed by him: Big Bear Root Beer, Lemon Cola, and Los Angeles Seltzer. If you're thirsty, the soda shop is well worth a visit.

SWEET THINGS

THE REFRESHER
SOFT DRINKS

21 22 23 24 25 26   29 30 32 33 34 35 37 38 39 40

A 200

NO EMPLOYEE DISCOUNT ON BOTTLED DRINKS!!!
PLEASE SIGN IN & OUT!

NO CELL PHONES, CD PLAYERS OR RADIOS
ALLOWED AT THE REFRESHER!!!

Big Bear Root Beer Float

The Bennett family has had a cabin on Big Bear Lake, nestled in the San Bernardino Mountains, for over three decades. Scott's handcrafted Big Bear Root Beer pays tribute to "Life up the Hill," as it says on the label. The soda is old-style draft and uses molasses as a dominant flavor. Pick up a pint of Bennett's ice cream to make the perfect root beer float!

SERVES 4

1 pint good-quality vanilla ice cream

2 bottles (16 ounces each) Big Bear Root Beer, very cold

Put 1 generous scoop of ice cream into each of 4 frozen fountain glasses or big mugs. Set the glasses on small plates to catch any overflow, and slowly fill the glasses with root beer. This will turn to foam. Keep pouring until the glass is full. The glasses will probably spill over—that's part of the fun! Serve the floats with straws and parfait spoons.

• •

Farmers Market folklore hints that this small shop was likely the cage that housed the renowned Gilmore Lion, which was the branded mascot for Gilmore Oil. In some Hollywood gossip, the Gilmore Lion is believed to have been the inspiration for Leo, the iconic MGM lion.

• •

T TEA SHOP

STALL
212

T Tea Shop is, quite literally, a small miracle. In a small shop, the scope of tea experience is huge. You'll find more than 250 varieties of teas here, from diverse blends of green teas, black teas, white teas, and herbals. Imports galore fill the shop, which offers an abundance of teas from Ceylon, Japan, India, and China, among other exotic sources. Whether to calm or to energize, to soothe or to satisfy, owner Young Min (see page 65) takes pride in her offerings and is happy to recommend and to help find the tea best for her customer. She recognizes tea's healthful benefits and praises the difference it makes to the body and soul. She believes if tea becomes part of a daily diet, one will sleep well, lose weight, have better circulation and digestion, and just be an all around better-balanced person.

Besides selling the various types, sold loose and by package, Young Min also acknowledges and respects the art of drinking tea and enjoying it properly. Hence, she offers an extensive collection of different accessories, from the traditional to the whimsical. Patrons can have their pick of infusers, teapots, mugs, cups and saucers, or cozies and trivets. So whatever time of day, whichever type of tea, visit T and take time to stop, sip, and savor.

= 茶 = TEA

#212

tea and beyond

ROYAL CHRSYANTHEMUM
719
$2.85/oz

CHAMOMILE
#701 $1.85/oz

PEPPERMINT LEAF
704
$1.85/oz

ROSE BUDS
705
$5.33/oz

PINK ROSE
$5.55/oz

Green Tea Smoothie

When you absolutely need something sweet, try this super-powered smoothie. It tastes like green tea ice cream in a drink. This emerald smoothie uses *matcha* powder to invigorate and satisfy the senses. It is a perfect refreshing smoothie with all the health benefits and great taste of green tea. T whips them up on the spot for their enlightened customers.

SERVES 2

2 cups plain soy milk

¼ cup honey

1 tablespoon *matcha* green tea powder (see Note)

2 cups ice cubes

Combine all of the ingredients in a blender. Puree until the ice has broken down and the smoothie is thick and green, about 1 minute. Pour into tall glasses and serve.

Ingredient Note—*Matcha*

Matcha is a powdered green tea from Japan that can be made as a tea or used as an ingredient. With *matcha*, whole tea leaves are consumed, not just the brewed water, as with other teas. To naturally produce a tea so green, the farmers cover the tea plants with bamboo mats several weeks prior to harvest. This step increases chlorophyll content and turns the leaves dark green. The leaves are then dried and ground into *matcha* powder. Rich in antioxidants, both green tea and *matcha* are renowned for their healthful detoxifying properties.

THEE'S CONTINENTAL PASTRIES

STALL
316

"Hear ye, hear ye. Get thee to Thee's Continental Pastries!" should be the flavorful cry of this divine European-style bakery, the best of its kind in Los Angeles. As they say, the apple doesn't fall far from the tree. Owner Bill Thee is the son of a baker. His father had a wholesale bakery in Los Angeles and was known for his signature spiced fruit-cake. Bill started working for his dad in the bakery after school when he was eight years old. Although Bill Sr. wanted his son to take over his bakery, Bill Jr. longed to be closer to the customer and decided the wholesale baking business was not the right fit. As a result, in his early twenties, he packed his bags and headed abroad to study pastry arts in Germany and Switzerland. There he found a passion for

pastries and cakes with a fine European flair. When he returned to Los Angeles, he worked in top bakeries throughout the city before he had the opportunity at the Market to buy Humphries Bakery (see sidebar) in 1981, which he revamped to match his accumulated experience and tastes.

What is the key ingredient to Thee's sweet success? The quality of the goods and the care in the preparation—pure butter, fresh whole eggs, and real cream all come together to create decadent delicacies with international flair. Homemade custards and buttercream frostings are Thee's specialties. At holiday time, Bill bakes up the European big guns and constructs eye-stopping three-tiered gingerbread houses, bûche de noël yule-log cakes, towers of croquembouche, and, of course, his father's famous fruitcake. Anything and everything at Thee's Continental Bakery is a much-appreciated indulgence, where quality is always the first ingredient.

This space once housed another beloved bakery; the Humphery brothers opened their bakery in 1948 and cleverly called it "Humphries"—a plural play on words. In the '50s, famed cake decorator and figure-piping artist John McNamara came on board. John is credited with creating the elaborate Pink Elephant Cake, with elephants made of pink frosting crawling all over it and crowned with a bottle of Champagne. Bill Thee still decorates the famous Pink Elephant Cake by hand in the window of the bakery for all to see. Not surprisingly, the cake is most popular for New Year's Eve and twenty-first birthdays.

Delcos

Similar to the famed Jewish pastry rugelach, these bite-size gems are made with a rich cream-cheese dough and provide a flaky purse for almost any fruit filling. There is no sugar in the dough but a light sprinkling on top of the cookie.

MAKES 2 DOZEN COOKIES

1 cup (2 sticks) unsalted butter, at room temperature

1 package (8 ounces) cream cheese, at room temperature

2 cups all-purpose flour, plus more for dusting

½ teaspoon salt

1 cup apricot or raspberry jam

Melted unsalted butter for brushing

Sugar for sprinkling

Put the butter and cream cheese in the bowl of a standing electric mixer fitted with a paddle attachment. (Alternatively, place in a large bowl and use a handheld electric mixer.) Turn the mixer on medium-high speed and cream together until very smooth and lump free. Add the 2 cups flour and salt and continue to beat until a soft dough forms. Divide the dough into 2 balls, flatten into disks, wrap in plastic, and refrigerate for at least 2 hours or up to overnight.

Preheat the oven to 350°F. Line 2 baking pans with parchment paper.

Using a floured rolling pin, roll a disk of dough out on a heavily floured work surface into a rectangle about ⅛ inch thick. The dough will start to soften up pretty quickly. Using a sharp knife or pizza cutter, cut the dough into 12 three-inch squares, then mist or lightly brush the surface with water to act as a glue to hold the cookies together. Put about 1 teaspoon of the jam in the center of the dough squares. Fold 2 corners toward the center, forming a diamond, and pinch to seal. Brush the cookies with melted butter, sprinkle with sugar, and transfer to a prepared baking pan. Repeat with the second dough disk.

Bake until golden brown, about 20 minutes. Let cool completely. Store in a tightly sealed container for up to 3 days.

243

Meringue Cookies

These delicate and airy cookies will have you on cloud nine. They're a favorite for people with a sweet tooth who don't want the richness of butter, egg yolks, and flour. As an insider tip, baker Bill Thee points out that egg whites right out of the refrigerator will not whip well. It's best to bring egg whites to room temperature before beating so they whip faster and fluffier. Meringues are very sensitive to humidity, so avoid making them on a damp day.

MAKES 2 DOZEN COOKIES

4 large egg whites, at room temperature	½ cup coarsely chopped walnuts
½ teaspoon cream of tartar	1 cup miniature chocolate chips
½ cup granulated sugar	½ cup confectioners' sugar, sifted

Preheat the oven to 250°F. Line 2 baking pans with parchment paper.

In a clean bowl, using a handheld electric mixer, whip the egg whites on low speed until foamy. Add the cream of tartar, raise the speed to medium, and beat until soft peaks form.

With the mixer running, gradually add the granulated sugar, a little at a time. Beat until the egg whites are stiff and glossy. Add the nuts and chocolate and continue to mix until evenly distributed. Fold in the confectioners' sugar with a rubber spatula until well blended.

Dollop spoonfuls of the meringue onto the baking pans, or use a pastry bag with a star tip. Bake for 1 hour. Turn off the heat and leave the meringues in the oven. Let the meringues cool and completely dry out, at least 3 hours. Meringues are ready when the surface is dry to the touch and can be removed cleanly off the paper. Store at room temperature in an airtight container to keep them crisp for up to 7 days.

ULTIMATE NUT & CANDY CO.

STALL
522

Sweet-tooth junkies and savory souls rejoice! Sugar and salt goodies abound at the Ultimate Nut & Candy Co. Originally known as the Magic Nut when it first opened at the Market in 1949, its delicious dilemmas now also include chocolate truffles and turtles, golden caramel corn, and brittle. The shop also carries candies that are made and enjoyed around the globe, featuring candied fruits from Australia, nougat from Spain, and Brazilian toffee. General store favorites like gumdrops, licorice whips, and saltwater taffy add an old-fashioned touch to the offerings. Whatever their choice, customers know that "ultimate" is key in the quality, service, and integrity of all that entices at this colorful stand brimming with sweets. Items are so popular that those who can't make it to the Market regularly (but remain in need of an ongoing nut or candy fix) can rest assured that their favorite indulgences are also available by mail order on the Ultimate Nut & Candy Web site.

SWEET THINGS

Lemongrass-and-Ginger Truffles

Chocolate truffles are a rich, decadent treat with a special elegance all their own. This exotic confection is a seductive blend of sweet and spice, with its inspired mixture of fresh ginger and lemongrass, enveloped in the finest dark chocolate.

MAKES 16 TRUFFLES

10 ounces bittersweet chocolate, plus 8 ounces for coating the truffles

2 tablespoons unsalted butter, at room temperature

1 cup heavy cream

1 tablespoon light corn syrup

1-inch piece fresh ginger, peeled and sliced

1 stalk lemongrass, white part only, sliced

1 cup Dutch process cocoa powder, sifted

Using a serrated knife, finely chop the 10 ounces chocolate and put in a heat-proof bowl. Add the butter. Set aside.

Pour the cream and corn syrup into a large pot over medium heat. Add the ginger and lemongrass. Bring to a boil. Remove from the heat, cover, and let steep for at least 20 minutes to infuse the flavors. Return to a boil over medium heat.

Strain the hot cream mixture through a fine-mesh strainer over the chocolate and butter. Discard the solids. Let stand for 2 minutes. Using a rubber spatula, stir gently in a circular motion, starting in the middle of bowl and working outward until all of the chocolate is melted and completely smooth. Refrigerate until firm, at least 2 hours.

Line a baking pan with parchment paper.

Using a melon baller or tablespoon, scoop out balls of the chilled chocolate mixture, roll into uniform balls with your hands, and put on the prepared pan. If the chocolate begins to warm up and soften as you work, return to the refrigerator for 10 minutes. After forming all of the truffles, chill the pan in the refrigerator for 15 minutes to harden the chocolate again.

Create a double boiler to melt the chocolate for the truffle coating: Put the remaining 8 ounces of chopped chocolate in a heat-proof bowl. Fill a pot halfway with water and bring to a simmer over medium heat. Set the bowl of chocolate over the pot, without letting the bottom touch. Stir the chocolate occasionally with a rubber spatula until it melts. Remove from the heat. Continue to stir as the chocolate begins to cool to 90°F on a candy thermometer.

Put the cocoa powder on a plate or in a small bowl.

Working with 1 at a time, dip a truffle into the melted chocolate. Remove with a fork, letting the excess chocolate drip back into the pot. Roll the truffles in the cocoa until well coated. Let set on a baking pan for at least 1 hour.

Store the truffles in an airtight container. They are best when served at room temperature. If refrigerated, remove 30 minutes before serving.

247

THREE DOG BAKERY

In 1989, three dogs (Sarah, Dottie, and Gracie), two guys (Mark Beckloff and Dan Dye), and one fifty-nine cent biscuit cutter joined forces to create Three Dog Bakery—the world's original bakery for dogs. Through trial and error, Mark and Dan managed to create healthful food that was appealing to fussy-eater dogs, with everyday ingredients. Peanut butter, wheat flour, honey, fruits, and vegetables were mixed together to produce the delicious all-natural, oven-baked treats. Soon, all their furry friends were enjoying fresh-baked delights that not only tasted good, but were good for them. And so Mark and Dan opened the first Three Dog Bakery retail store in Kansas City that put the "wow" into bow wow.

Ten years later, California native and avid dog lover Mark Bodnar, walked into the flagship Three Dog Bakery and walked out $300 poorer, loaded down with goodies for his dog, neighbors' dogs, and friends' dogs. He was immediately intrigued by the concept and knew the gourmet "barkery" would be a smash hit in Los Angeles. The city is, after all, a Shangri-La for man's best friend and has seen its fair share of doggie indulgence and puppy pampering. After a bare bones beginning, Mark now owns three Three Dog Bakeries in the Los Angeles area. The Farmers Market store opened in 2001 to Hollywood's top dogs who bark and beg for custom-designed cakes and treats for special occasions. Mark once created a four-tiered wedding cake for the "Bow-Vows" of two Labs at the Beverly Hills Hotel and often makes kosher cakes for "Bark Mitzvahs" when pubescent pups turn thirteen (that's almost two in people years). All of their products are baked on site, and the wholesome, close-to-the-earth ingredients are free of harsh chemicals and contain no artificial flavors, colors, or preservatives. In fact, these healthful treats are not just for our four-legged friends but also are loved by their owners and folks with dietary concerns, such as diabetes. To succeed, Mark has worked like a dog, but he says he wouldn't have it any other way.

Bow Wow Brownies

These brownies replace normal chocolate (which is toxic to dogs) with carob so pooches everywhere can enjoy the tasty treats their owners love. The largest order for one client was a hundred brownies for a Beverly Hills puppy pool party. Your chow hound will love them. Bone appétit!

MAKES 18 BROWNIES

Brownie Batter

½ cup vegetable shortening

2 tablespoons honey

4 large eggs

1 teaspoon pure vanilla extract

1 cup unbleached all-purpose flour

½ teaspoon baking powder

¼ cup carob powder

½ cup carob chips

Frosting

1 package (8 ounces) low-fat cream
   cheese, at room temperature

1 tablespoon carob powder

1 teaspoon pure vanilla extract

Preheat the oven to 350°F. Coat a 9-by-13-inch baking dish with nonstick cooking spray.

To make the brownie batter: In a large bowl, cream together the shortening and honey. Add the eggs, vanilla, flour, baking powder, and carob powder. Beat well until the batter is smooth. Fold in the carob chips until evenly distributed.

Pour the brownie batter into the prepared pan. Bake until the brownies pull away from the sides of the pan slightly, about 25 minutes. Set aside to let cool completely.

To make the frosting: Combine the cream cheese, carob powder, and vanilla in a large bowl. Mix until light and well blended.

Spread the frosting over the cooled brownies and cut into squares. To store, cover with plastic wrap or transfer to a sealed container and refrigerate for up to 3 days.

Peanut Butter Pupovers

Many dogs find peanut butter treats irresistible, and even more so when they're fresh and homemade. These "popovers" are a four-legged favorite at Three Dog Bakery. Pups just can't wait to get their paws on these wholesome, delicious snacks. Be sure to use all-natural peanut butter to avoid excess salt, sugar, and additives.

MAKES 12 PUPOVERS

1 cup unbleached all-purpose flour

1 cup nonfat milk

2 large eggs

¼ cup all-natural creamy peanut butter

1 tablespoon vegetable oil

Preheat the oven to 475°F. Coat a standard 12-cup muffin pan with nonstick cooking spray.

In a large bowl, combine the flour, milk, eggs, and peanut butter. Using a handheld electric mixer, beat until thoroughly blended. Add the oil and beat for 1 minute longer.

Spoon the batter into the prepared muffin pan, filling each cup halfway. Bake for 15 minutes, then reduce the oven temperature to 350°F and continue to bake until puffed and golden, about 25 minutes.

A few minutes before removing them from the oven, prick the top of each pupover with a fork to release the steam. Let cool completely before serving to Fido or Fifi. Store at room temperature in an airtight container for up to 3 days.

251

SWEET THINGS

Index

Table of Equivalents

The exact equivalents in the following tables have been rounded for convenience.

Liquid/Dry Measurements

U.S.	Metric
¼ teaspoon	1.25 milliliters
½ teaspoon	2.5 milliliters
1 teaspoon	5 milliliters
1 tablespoon (3 teaspoons)	15 milliliters
1 fluid ounce (2 tablespoons)	30 milliliters
¼ cup	60 milliliters
⅓ cup	80 milliliters
½ cup	120 milliliters
1 cup	240 milliliters
1 pint (2 cups)	480 milliliters
1 quart (4 cups, 32 ounces)	960 milliliters
1 gallon (4 quarts)	3.84 liters
1 ounce (by weight)	28 grams
1 pound	448 grams
2.2 pounds	1 kilogram

Lengths

U.S.	Metric
⅛ inch	3 millimeters
¼ inch	6 millimeters
½ inch	12 millimeters
1 inch	2.5 centimeters

Oven Temperature

Fahrenheit	Celsius	Gas
250	120	½
275	140	1
300	150	2
325	160	3
350	180	4
375	190	5
400	200	6
425	220	7
450	230	8
475	240	9
500	260	10